Rocks
and Minerals
of Nunavut

Jurate Gertzbein

T0126172

Published by Inhabit Media Inc.
www.inhabitmedia.com

Inhabit Media Inc. (Iqaluit), P.O. Box 11125, Iqaluit, Nunavut, X0A 1H0
(Toronto), 146A Orchard View Blvd., Toronto, Ontario, M4R 1C3

We acknowledge the support of the Canada Council for the Arts for our publishing program.

Printed and bound in Hong Kong.

Photography	Danny Christopher
	Mélanie Houde
Stock Photographs	Royal Ontario Museum
	Shutterstone.com
Illustrations	Danny Christopher

Library and Archives Canada Cataloguing in Publication

Gertzbein, Jurate
        Rocks and minerals of Nunavut / Jurate Gertzbein.

Includes bibliographical references and index.
ISBN 978-1-927095-10-2

        1. Rocks--Nunavut--Identification. 2. Minerals--Nunavut--Identification. 3. Geology--Nunavut. I. Title.

QE446.N85G47 2012   552.09719'5   C2012-900588-6

NBES

Nunavut

Canadä

Canada Council Conseil des Arts
for the Arts   du Canada

Department of Education
Department of Culture, Language, Elders and Youth

Canadian Heritage
Parks Canada
Environment Canada - Canadian Wildlife Service
Canada Council for the Arts

Rocks
and Minerals
of Nunavut

Jurate Gertzbein

INHABIT
MEDIA

Acknowledgements

I am indebted to Carolyn Mallory for long hours of proofreading and editing, and to Gwen Frankton for an early review of the project. In particular, Carolyn's advice on the experience of writing *Common Plants of Nunavut* was invaluable to me. For assistance and support, thanks to Neil Christopher, Mark Mallory, and Tony Romito. Without these people, this book would not be a reality.

A large thank you also goes out to NBES for helping to fund a book on this topic and to Jim Noble and Gwen Frankton for their continued belief in this series of books in Nunavut. A sincere thank you to the team for inviting me to write this book. I am honoured to have been a part of this first geoscience book in the Inuktitut language.

Dedication

My husband, Paul Gertzbein, passed away during the writing of this book. His love buoyed me and his support of the project underlined the importance of going on with the writing after his death.

Biography

Jurate Gertzbein has written or contributed to over fifteen books, including *Roadside Geology of Ontario* and *Rock ON: Geology of Ontario*. She had a thirty-year career in geology working as an exploration geologist, interpretive geologist, prospector, mine inspector, and mineral development advisor for both provincial and federal governments. Jurate was a director for both the Northwestern Ontario Prospectors and Manitoba Prospectors and Developers Associations, and was the spokesperson for the Ontario Prospectors' Assistance Program. Even in retirement she stays active in geology by prospecting for gemstones and volunteering at geology events. Jurate splits her time between a remote lakeside camp in northwestern Ontario and a historic rock house in the Hill Country of Texas.

Table of Contents

MINERAL DESCRIPTIONS

ROCK DESCRIPTIONS

Introduction

In this practical handbook, students of science and geology, prospectors, and those curious about the Earth will discover the world of minerals and rocks. This guide outlines how to classify rocks, as well as the substances they are made of and the processes through which they were formed. This handbook also provides some fundamentals of geology, which is the formal study of rocks and minerals, along with a description of the traditional and modern uses of these resources, and where these minerals can be found in Nunavut.

With over 3,800 minerals on the planet, this book focuses on the most common minerals and rocks occurring in Nunavut. Luckily, these are also the most common worldwide. A few very rare minerals are included, such as diamond and sapphire, due to their new-found importance in Nunavut.

The introductory chapters set up the three main rock types on Earth and describe some of the processes at work in their formation. A rock is made of a variety of minerals, and geologists have created a way to name rocks based on the types and amounts of minerals in them. Readers will learn how to identify minerals based on this handbook and their own investigation.

There are two main approaches to identifying your rock samples. The first approach requires following the process outlined in the flow charts on pages 23 to 25. Once the potential rock name is determined, readers can turn to the page associated with that rock. Check to see how closely the specimen matches the description, and note whether the minerals in the rock are listed in the write-up. The second approach is to first determine what minerals are in the hand specimen and in what proportion they occur, in order to flip through the rock pages to find a match.

Under the mineral descriptions are chemical formulas, which are like the DNA or fingerprint of a mineral. These chemical formulas give scientists most of the information required to understand a particular substance. For the non-specialist, these formulas also provide some clues as to which family of minerals is being examined. Sometimes minerals that are found together all contain the same particular element, and identifying these common elements is important.

You will see that each rock description contains an alternate name. Usually the alternate names are very old names, from Latin, that have fallen largely out of favour. Some of the alternate names may now cause confusion because they were created before the

Photo: Mélanie Houde

chemistry of the mineral was known. The more modern names arose out of better scientific investigation. Scientists use specific terminology—this can be confusing to the beginner, but the glossary provides definitions. Any word in bold has a definition found in the glossary at the end of the book. If read chronologically (introductory chapters first), readers will be in a better position to understand the terminology in the mineral and rock description pages. With the basics presented in this book, students, prospectors, and casual geologists alike will be ready to learn about **fossils**, glaciology, landforms, tectonics (movement of the **crust** of the Earth), hydrology, the environment that exists above the **bedrock**, and mineral **deposits**.

Mineral deposits are unusual concentrations of minerals that have interest or value. Scientists study many rare minerals simply to better understand the planet and its processes. Prospectors, exploration companies, and mining companies search for mineral deposits that have monetary and industry value.

The value of a mineral **occurrence** will depend on many factors: the concentration of the mineral; the ease of its extraction from the bedrock; the demand for this mineral; the cost of the milling and refining; the environmental cost (how damaging the extraction will be to the natural environment); marketing; shipping costs; and a host of other considerations.

The use of minerals and rocks has always been important to the survival of Inuit in the Arctic. For example, small-scale mining has occurred for a very long time. Traditional uses of rocks and minerals include the carving of soapstone for *qulluit* and the use of copper for blades.

Minerals have been valued by man since the beginning of time, and many people feel a strong spiritual connection to minerals, rocks, and landforms. Every society recognizes the inherent beauty and usefulness of minerals, while individuals treasure their pendants, talismans, and **gemstones** for sacred and personal reasons. Minerals are part of almost everything we use in modern society, from eyeglasses to computer components, paint, and vitamins. So let's enjoy this journey into the world of geology as we recognize the beauty and value of Nunavut's rocks and minerals.

Part One

What Is a Mineral?

A mineral is a substance that occurs in nature and is formed by geologic processes. For example, when a hot liquid travels along a crack in the Earth's crust, the liquid gradually cools and tiny **crystals** form. This process creates minerals. A mineral has a defined chemical composition, that is, a regular pattern to its **atoms**. Atoms are the smallest particles produced in a chemical reaction. Although the chemical composition of a mineral may vary somewhat, it is always within a known range. The arrangement of atoms forms a regular and repeating three-dimensional network, or crystal system. This **atomic structure** leads to a set of physical properties, such as the colour and **hardness**, by which means we are often able to identify minerals.

Most mineral names end in *-ite* and *-lite*. This is from a Greek-derived suffix *lithos*, which means *stone*. The first part of the name may describe an obvious property of the mineral. Alternatively, the name may reflect the location where the mineral was first found. The discoverer of the mineral, or a chemist or mineralogist, may also be honoured in the mineral's name.

Over 3,800 minerals have been discovered on Earth, and we know that minerals comprise meteorites and the moon. Each year about fifty new minerals are identified. Without minerals there would be no planet Earth. All the materials that humans need for life are derived, either directly or indirectly, from minerals. Plants that we eat grow in **soil**, a product of the **erosion** of rocks, which contains mineral nutrients. Bones in our bodies need calcium to grow strong, and the vitamins we take contain many minerals, including calcium. Metals are used to make tools and form the foundation of industry. Minerals are vital to life and our very existence on Earth.

Part Two

What Is a Gem?

A gem is the most prized type of mineral. Usually a gem is defined by its scarcity, its beautiful colour, and the extreme hardness of its surface. Gems are widely used in jewellery and for ornamental purposes.

When a gem is cut and polished it is referred to as a gemstone. Precious stones include diamonds, emeralds, rubies, and sapphires. Semi-precious stones include amethyst, topaz, tourmaline, and garnet.

Skilled cutters know how to accentuate the colour, brilliance, and dispersion (how light sparkles with a rainbow effect from inside the stone), and how to downplay any negative features of the gemstone.

Part Three

Mineral Identification

Mineral identification can be quite a complicated procedure, even for experts. However, there are some qualities to look for that make the task easier.

A variety of observations can be made to help with identification. Superficial observation includes identifying the colour, **lustre**, and **habit** of the mineral. Secondary characteristics include its **streak**, hardness, fracture, **cleavage**, **specific gravity**, and other attributes defined below.

Chemical elements, which are the building blocks of all materials, and the atomic structure (how atoms combine into **molecules**) of a mineral, are invisible characteristics, yet it is these unseen chemical properties that constitute the physical appearance of the mineral.

Because some properties are not observable, and some minerals are too complex to be easily identified, the assistance of a geologist (an expert on minerals, rocks, and earth science) or a mineral collector may be required.

Colour

The colour of a mineral often attracts our attention first. Most minerals of the same type can occur in a variety of colours, so colour is not the sole basis for identification. There are also many minerals that are white or colourless, requiring other tests to be done in order to identify them. The **tarnish** that may coat a mineral is often a characteristic colour as well.

Photo: Shutterstone.com

A colourful example of serpentine

How light is absorbed into a mineral determines the colour the eye sees. For example, a black crystal absorbs all the light entering it, whereas a white grain allows the full spectrum of light to pass through it. Observe the mineral's colour in natural light and on a fresh surface to determine its true colour.

Lustre

Lustre is the way that light is reflected off a mineral's surface. Lustre is independent of colour. The main determination is based on whether the specimen is metallic or non-metallic.

If the mineral is non-metallic, it must then be determined whether the mineral is dull, earthy, pearly, **vitreous** (glassy), greasy, waxy, silky, **resinous** (like amber), or **adamantine** (brilliant and shiny, like a diamond).

Habit

The habit of a mineral is the characteristic form or shape in which it appears. **Equant** minerals have the same diameter in every direction, so they look quite round, for example. **Prismatic** minerals have long and narrow crystals. A mineral that is **massive** has no clear form or structure. Minerals can also appear in the following forms: **dendritic** (plantlike or skeletal); bladed (like a knife blade); **acicular** (long and needlelike); **fibrous** (hairlike); **botryoidal** (resembling a cluster of grapes); **reniform** (rounded and kidney-shaped); **druse** (having crystals growing in a cavity); **geode** (having a cavity filled in with minerals); **crusted** (having a thin overgrowth); **tabular** (long and wide but quite thin, like a table); **columnar** (columnlike); and earthy (crumbly and powdery).

There are also natural puzzles called **pseudomorphs**. A pseudomorph is a mineral formation with a crystal shape that is not characteristic of that mineral. It is formed through the dissolution of one crystal in a solid rock, followed by the crystallization of a second mineral, thus having one mineral replaced by another.

Acicular

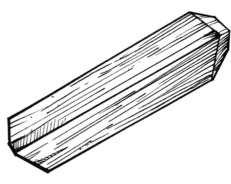

Prismatic

Equant

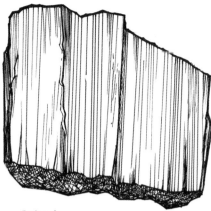

Striated

Tabular

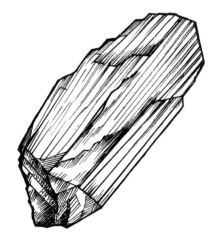

Bladed

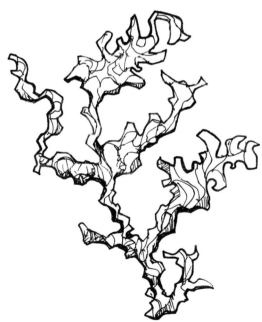

Dendritic

Streak

The streak is the colour of a mineral's powder and it is a more consistent test than notation of the mineral's colour. A streak can be obtained by rubbing the specimen across the surface of an unglazed porcelain tile. If an unglazed tile is unavailable, the unglazed underside of a porcelain dish or the bottom of a vase may be used. For a very hard mineral, crush a small amount with a geological hammer and transfer the powder to white paper.

All white and light-coloured minerals will produce a white streak, and very soft minerals will leave a good streak on paper. All metallic minerals will produce coloured, black, or metallic streaks. The streak test is therefore very useful with metallic minerals. Many other dark minerals will leave a grey streak.

Hardness

One test of a mineral's hardness is its resistance to being scratched. In 1822, Friedrich **Mohs** devised a relative scale consisting of ten minerals: (1) talc, (2) gypsum, (3) calcite, (4) fluorite, (5) apatite, (6) orthoclase, (7) quartz, (8) topaz, (9) corundum, and (10) diamond. A mineral with a higher number is harder and will leave a scratch on a mineral of a lower number. Also, a mineral of an unknown hardness can be rubbed with minerals of known hardness in order to determine its position on the scale.

Everyday items can be used to test hardness. A fingernail has a hardness of 2.5. Other examples include a copper penny (3.5), a knife blade or safety pin (5.5), glass (6), and a steel file (6–6.5).

Once scratched, a mineral may leave powder behind, which should be blown away. A **hand lens** (magnifying glass) is required to see any resulting scratch. Keep in mind that a scratch will be permanent, so this test should be made in an inconspicuous spot.

Cleavage

Cleavage is the way a mineral breaks along well-defined planes of weakness. Typically these planes are between layers of atoms where the electrical forces that keep a molecule together are the weakest. A **cleavage plane** is smoother and more reflective than a crystal face. Often cleavage planes can be recognized by the simultaneous reflection of light from numerous parallel surfaces, all at different levels. This flash is quite distinctive.

Cleavage planes may appear inside **translucent** (partially clear or see-through) or transparent minerals as slightly milky planes. Cleavage can also be revealed by gentle hammering or picking with a sharp point.

It is important to note if the cleavage is perfect (very well-developed); distinct (well-developed); indistinct (somewhat developed); poor (poorly developed); or absent. More than one cleavage direction is sometimes present, and if cleavages intersect, the angle between the two planes is important to record. Two very similar minerals, amphibole and pyroxene, can easily be distinguished by their cleavage angles.

Photo: Shutterstone.com

There is also a property called **parting**, which is the tendency of a mineral to break along weak surfaces, such as a **twin plane** (a plane in which one crystal is reflected into its twin). Most minerals do not display a parting, but in a few minerals it is quite common.

Amphibole cleaving

Fracture

If a specimen is struck with a hammer and breaks, revealing uneven surfaces, then the mineral has a fracture. If the resulting break is shaped like a clamshell, it is called **conchoidal**. A **hackly** fracture is sharp and jagged, like broken metal. A **splintery fracture** resembles fractured wood. An **earthy fracture** looks like a break across hard soil. Occasionally the break will have no pattern, and is then called uneven.

Specific Gravity

The specific gravity (SG) compares the weight of a mineral with the weight of an equal volume of water. A mineral with an SG of 2.5 is 2.5 times heavier than water. Some apparatus is required to measure SG; however, for the purpose of basic mineral identification, the approximate SG or the density can be assessed by holding one mineral of known value in one hand and comparing it to the unknown mineral. Of course, it is important to compare two specimens of similar volume.

Light minerals have an SG of less than two, while normal minerals range from two to four. Heavy minerals are greater than four. Most light-coloured rock-forming minerals have an SG of about 2.7, while pyrite and other ore minerals, at an SG of six, are heavy. Gold tips the scales at 19.3.

Crystal System

If a regular geometric shape in the specimen is observed, the crystal system to which the mineral belongs can easily be determined. There are six main systems based on **symmetry**. A plane of symmetry divides a crystal into two halves, one half being an identical mirror image of the other. An **axis** is a line about which the crystal can be rotated and still reveal symmetry. In normal hand specimens, the crystal system cannot be easily determined, but museums contain many perfect crystals with symmetry. The following chart describes the six main systems used to identify crystals.

	System	Description	Axes (length and angle)
	Cubic	cube (six-sided), octahedra (eight-sided), dodecahedra (twelve-sided)	three axes of equal lengths, all perpendicular to one another
	Tetragonal	usually more elongated than a cube	three axes all perpendicular to one another; two axes of equal lengths; principal axis of different length
	Orthorhombic	prisms and flattened tabular form	three axes all of different lengths and all perpendicular to one another
	Monoclinic	common; lower degree of symmetry than cubic	three axes all of different lengths; two axes perpendicular; third axis is inclined
	Triclinic	least symmetrical	all three axes are of different lengths and are all inclined to one another
	Hexagonal and Trigonal	two systems grouped together due to similar axes of symmetry	three out of four axes lie on the same plane, are of equal lengths, and intersect at 120°; fourth axis not the same length and not perpendicular; hexagonal has six-sided cross-section of prismatic base; trigonal has three-sided cross-section of prismatic base

Deformability

The tenacity (strength) of a mineral is a clear diagnostic feature. Some minerals, like the mica group, are elastic and will return to their original shape after bending. Minerals that take on a new shape upon bending are considered flexible. **Ductile** minerals (usually the metals) can be made into wires. A malleable mineral is capable of being hammered into thin sheets. If a mineral can be cut by a knife to produce a shaving, it is said to be **sectile**. A **brittle** mineral is easily reduced into fragments by hammer, or by crushing with a light force.

Twinning

When two or more crystals of the same species have grown together in a nonparallel, symmetrical fashion, this is called **twinning**. Two common types of twinning are contact (twinned crystals that appear to be somewhat overlapping) and **interpenetrant twins** (when one twin appears to have grown all the way through the other). The mineral gypsum often forms a **swallowtail** (resembling a swallow's tail) twin.

The key to recognizing twinning is to find re-entrant angles (like V's notched into the crystal), as some minerals have common and distinctive twin patterns.

Transparency

Transparency is the way light passes through a mineral. If objects are visible through the mineral, it is transparent. If light passes through, but an object cannot be seen clearly, the mineral is translucent. **Opaque** minerals do not allow any light through.

Calcite is easily identified by its double **refraction**. Double refraction occurs when a beam of light splits into two and each part takes a different path through the crystal. Thus a double image is visible through a calcite specimen.

Iridescence is an interference phenomenon (occurring when the path of light is obstructed), in which the atomic structure of the mineral acts like a prism, causing light to split into bands of colour. Rainbow-coloured reflections seem to play as the specimen is turned. More simply, iridescence can be defined as the appearance of luminous colours that seem to change when seen from different angles.

Understanding the way light refracts as it enters, travels through, and exits a crystal is important to those who work with gemstones. Diamonds, for example, are cut into a specific pattern to allow for the greatest refraction, which creates an astonishing array of colours and flashes (known as "fire").

Fluorescence

The **fluorescent** property of some minerals was first described by Sir George Stokes in 1852. He shone shortwave electromagnetic irradiation (a particular wavelength of light) at minerals and found that some minerals emitted a visible light. The mineral fluorite is named after this property. Another common fluorescent mineral is calcite. An ultraviolet light is the basic tool required for this test.

Magnetism

A few minerals have **magnetic** properties. To test for magnetism, tie a magnet to a string and hold it near the specimen to observe whether the magnet moves closer to the specimen. Small swing magnets can be used for this purpose. If a compass is available, place it on a table and let the needle come to rest. Then bring the specimen gradually closer to the needle and watch for any movement of the needle. Alternatively, crush some of the mineral into a powder, place the powder on a piece of paper, move a magnet underneath the paper, and watch to see whether the grains move around.

Solubility in Acid

Geologists often use a diluted hydrochloric acid solution in a dropper bottle to test for solubility. Some minerals will break down instantly in acid and release carbon dioxide **gas** in the form of bubbles. This property of **effervescence** is clearly observed in calcite and aragonite. Dolomite will dissolve, but does not produce fizz. Nepheline will not dissolve, but is altered and will develop a gel on its surface.

Only work with acids when assisted by a knowledgeable geologist, chemist, or expert chemical scientist!

Part Four

Mineral Classes

All minerals can be assigned to a mineral class based on crystal chemistry, that is, the chemical components and the crystal structure. Crystals are the regular geometric shapes that minerals can form. When the word **radical** is used in the text that follows, it means a group of atoms (the basic unit of a chemical element) that behave together in a very stable way, thus resisting any chemical changes.

Silicates belong to the largest mineral class and make up more than 90% of the Earth's crust. Silicate minerals are typically hard and may have a glassy appearance. A few silicate minerals are very common around the world, but the majority of silicate minerals are quite rare. The silicate atomic structure, a tetrahedron, is a shape with four equilateral triangular faces (all three sides are of equal lengths). Silica and oxygen are the elements that make up the tetrahedra. The manner in which these tetrahedra are linked forms the basis of further subdivisions.

Native elements occur in a free, uncombined state (they are not mixed with other elements), and include metals (e.g., gold), **semimetals** (e.g., arsenic), and non-metals (e.g., sulphur). These metals are capable of being hammered into thin sheets, are malleable, and exhibit metallic lustre. Semimetals tend to be massive. Non-metals are transparent to translucent and form distinct crystals such as diamonds.

Sulphides, arsenides, tellurides, and sulphosalts are simple compounds, formed from either sulphur, selenium, or tellurium, respectively. Sulphides are soft, heavy, and brittle; contain a sulphur atom; and often display a metallic lustre. Arsenide minerals always contain an arsenic atom, while telluride minerals always have a telluride atom. Sulphosalts contain both a metal and a semimetal along with sulphur. Sulphosalts are rare, soft, heavy, and brittle.

Oxides and hydroxides are groups of metallic elements with oxygen and water, known as the hydroxyl radical. Oxides have a great range of colour, hardness, and transparency. The hydroxides are generally softer and less dense than the oxides.

Halides are compounds in which a halogen element (chlorine, fluorine, iodine, or bromine) is the only negatively charged **ion** (an electrically charged atom). These minerals are relatively soft, weak, and brittle. Many, like halite (more commonly called rock salt), will dissolve readily in water.

Carbonates are compounds of one or more metallic or semimetallic elements with the carbonate radical. A few carbonates display bright colours, but many are white, colourless, or transparent. Carbonates are soft.

Nitrates and borates are compounds made up of one or more metallic elements with the nitrate or borate radical. **Anhydrous** (without water) borates are dark in colour and heavy. **Hydrous** (with water) borates are brittle, relatively soft, and white, colourless, or transparent. Nitrates are easily dissolved in water and thus are only found under very dry conditions.

Sulphates are compounds made up of one or more metallic elements with the sulphate radical. Mostly light in colour, they are transparent to translucent. They are soft and fragile.

Phosphates, vanadates, and arsenates are compounds made up of metallic elements from phosphate, vanadate, and arsenate radicals. These minerals are brightly coloured, soft, and brittle, and form small, inconspicuous masses or crystals.

Tungstates, molybdates, and uranates are compounds made up of metallic elements from tungstate, molybdate, and uranate radicals. Generally heavy, soft, and brittle, these minerals are dark or vividly coloured purple, red, green, blue, yellow, or turquoise.

Scheelite: a tungstate

Part Five

What Is a Rock?

A rock is a natural grouping of minerals. A rock is either a large number of the same mineral, or two or more minerals. A grouping of minerals must form a large, solid body in order to be called a rock.

Unlike minerals, rocks cannot be identified by a simple test. Initially the external appearance and structure will determine the main rock type. Then only by careful examination of the minerals in the grouping can the rock name be given.

Understanding the formation of rocks also helps geologists locate **ore deposits**, which are large masses of useful minerals that can be profitably mined. As well, many types of scientists study features present in the rocks to learn about ancient climates and geography. Studying rocks also teaches us about the conditions of the environment at the time of rock formation.

Part Six

Classification of Rocks

Igneous Rocks

Igneous rocks are formed by the solidification of liquid **molten** rock, or **magma**. Magmas are less dense than crustal rock and therefore rise slowly from the **mantle** (the thick layer of the Earth between the crust and the core) and the lower crust. If crustal fractures are present in the mantle, the viscous liquid will follow those pathways. Magma that collects and solidifies within the crust forms rocks that are **intrusive**, while magma that erupts at the Earth's surface is **lava**, which pours out of fissures or volcanoes, forming **extrusive** (or **volcanic**) rocks. At shallow crustal levels, magma can solidify, and when this happens, the rocks are termed hypabyssal rocks.

Igneous rocks are hard and dense, with a massive texture (no particular form or structure). **Intrusive rocks** are typically coarse-grained because the magma cooled slowly, allowing for large crystal growth. Extrusive rocks are fine-grained because they cool and solidify rapidly.

Sedimentary Rocks

When **weathering** products of other rocks accumulate, **sedimentary** rocks are formed. Processes such as weathering, erosion, transport, and **deposition** all happen at the Earth's surface. As **sediments** collect in rivers, lakes, and seas, they can accumulate to a thickness of several kilometres. The weight of all this sediment exerts a great pressure on the lowermost layers, compacting and cementing them. **Detrital** rocks are derived from the mechanical weathering and transport of rock particles. **Biogenic** rocks are formed from the accumulation of animal skeletons or shells. Chemical sedimentary rocks form when a body of water becomes saturated (filled to capacity) with an element, and crystals precipitate.

In sedimentary rocks, a type of layering called bedding is usually prominent. Beds are formed due to the physical size sorting of grains. A bed formed from larger, heavier grains is usually in the bottom layer, while the smaller-grained beds form the upper layers. These layers can also be formed when the style of **sedimentation** changes due to alterations in the environmental conditions. Fossils are common types of sedimentary rocks, as are other geographical indicators, like ripple marks and mud cracks.

Metamorphic Rocks

Metamorphic rocks are formed from pre-existing rocks due to exposure to a different set of physical conditions, like temperature and pressure. Where and when great earth movements occur, such as **mountain-building**, vast areas of rock are affected by **regional metamorphism**. Due to stresses acting on the rock, as minerals **crystallize**, their long axes run perpendicular to the direction of the force. This force/stress/axis movement gives the rocks a distinct **foliation**, which means that the flat minerals are stacked. On a smaller scale, **contact metamorphism** occurs when the rocks surrounding an **intrusion** are altered by the intense heat. These rocks are identified by a "baked" appearance and a spotty and randomly oriented crystal texture. Rocks can also be affected by more than one type of metamorphism.

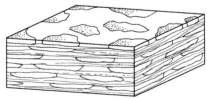

Foliation

The Rock Cycle

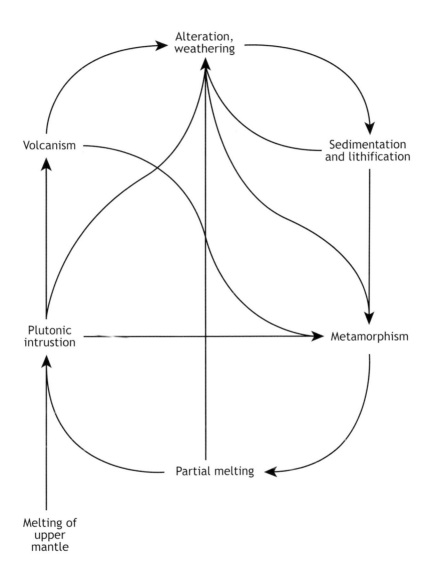

Part Eight

Identifying Rocks

When heading out onto the land to collect rocks and minerals, a few items are required: geologic hammer, goggles, chisel, knife, magnet, hand lens, sledgehammer, dilute hydrochloric acid (or vinegar), bags, marker, compass, GPS, notebook, pencil, knapsack, and maps. Be aware of tide schedules and always let someone know where you are going.

The best collecting locations are called **outcrops**, also known as bedrock, which are areas that stick up through the overlying cover of **glacial debris**. When glaciers melt they leave a lot of gravel and pebbles strewn about—this is what is known as glacial debris. To better identify minerals and textures in the rock, break off pieces with the hammer and investigate the fresh surface.

Step One:

Examine the entire outcrop. Is there layering? If so, it is probably a sedimentary rock. The appearance of fossils also indicates a sedimentary exposure. While studying and describing the fossils at the site is permitted, in Nunavut it is unlawful to remove fossils from their site of origin. Determine the location, note it down, and notify the Department of Culture, Language, Elders and Youth (CLEY) about the discovery. If the layering is strongly **folded** (crumpled like a messy blanket) and/or there is a mineral foliation, this is a metamorphic rock.

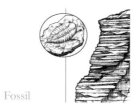

Fossil

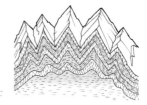

Folded metamorphic

If there is a random texture in the mineral grains it is probably an igneous rock. Volcanic rocks commonly are fine-grained and exhibit **flow textures** (bands displaying different minerals, colours, or textures formed by an igneous process).

Step Two:

Once it is determined whether the outcrop exposes igneous, sedimentary, or metamorphic rocks, turn to the appropriate flow chart, which will help identify the rock even further. Note that only the most common rocks are presented.

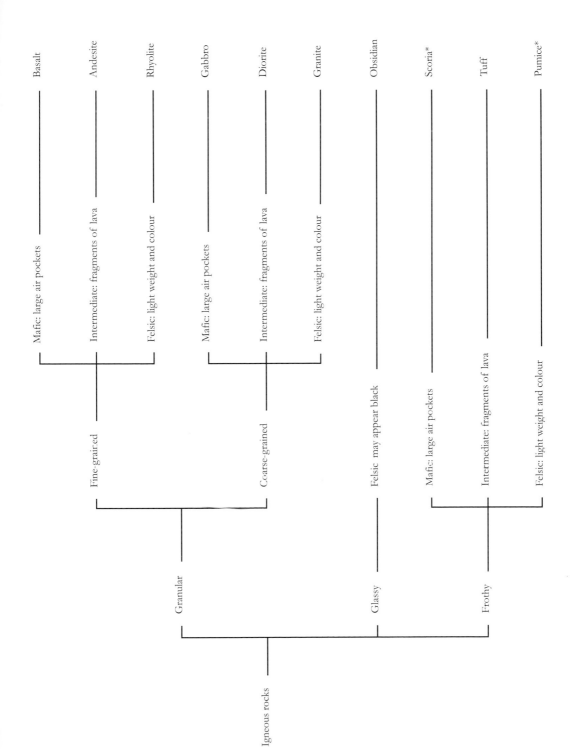

Igneous rocks
- Granular
  - Fine-grained
    - Mafic: large air pockets — Basalt
    - Intermediate: fragments of lava — Andesite
    - Felsic: light weight and colour — Rhyolite
  - Coarse-grained
    - Mafic: large air pockets — Gabbro
    - Intermediate: fragments of lava — Diorite
    - Felsic: light weight and colour — Granite
- Glassy
  - Felsic may appear black — Obsidian
- Frothy
  - Mafic: large air pockets — Scoria*
  - Intermediate: fragments of lava — Tuff
  - Felsic: light weight and colour — Pumice*

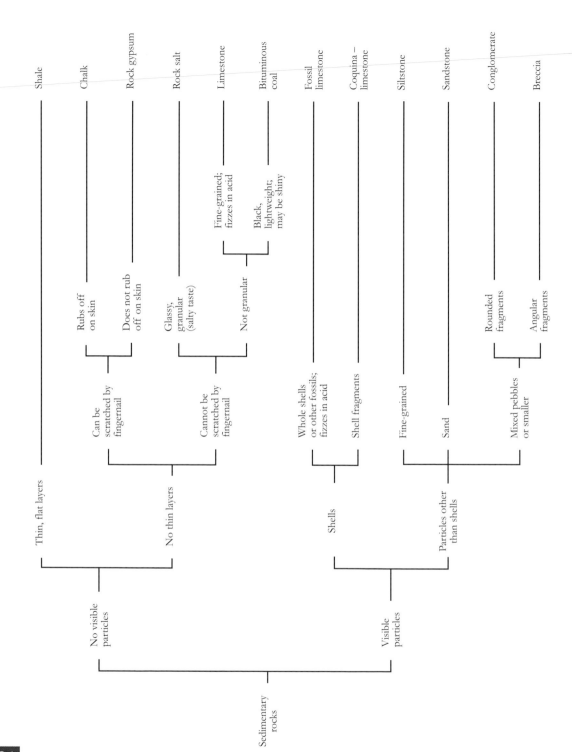

Shale

Chalk

Rock gypsum

Rock salt

Limestone

Bituminous coal

Fossil limestone

Coquina – limestone

Siltstone

Sandstone

Conglomerate

Breccia

Fine-grained; fizzes in acid

Black, lightweight; may be shiny

Rubs off on skin

Does not rub off on skin

Glassy, granular (salty taste)

Not granular

Rounded fragments

Angular fragments

Can be scratched by fingernail

Cannot be scratched by fingernail

Whole shells or other fossils; fizzes in acid

Shell fragments

Fine-grained

Sand

Mixed pebbles or smaller

Thin, flat layers

No thin layers

Shells

Particles other than shells

No visible particles

Visible particles

Sedimentary rocks

24

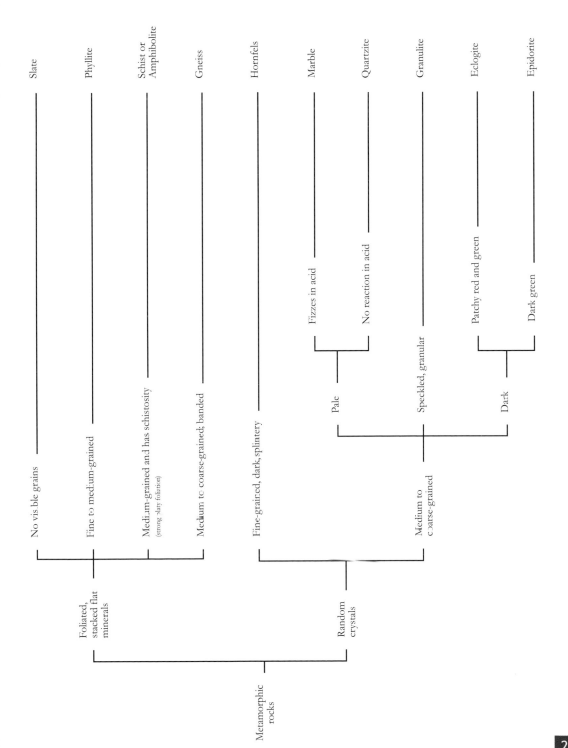

Metamorphic rocks

Foliated, stacked flat minerals
- No visible grains — Slate
- Fine to medium-grained — Phyllite
- Medium-grained and has schistosity (strong slaty foliation) — Schist or Amphibolite
- Medium to coarse-grained; banded — Gneiss

Random crystals
- Fine-grained, dark, splintery — Hornfels
- Medium to coarse-grained
  - Pale
    - Fizzes in acid — Marble
    - No reaction in acid — Quartzite
  - Speckled, granular — Granulite
  - Dark
    - Patchy red and green — Eclogite
    - Dark green — Epidorite

Part Twelve
Igneous Rock Settings

Plutonic (Intrusive) Environments

Pluto was the Greek god of the underworld, so it is appropriate that his name is used to describe igneous rocks that form within the Earth's crust (the thin outer layer). A **batholith** is a huge body of rock and may be hundreds of kilometres long. Many batholithic rocks are massive, whereas some are layered. It is only through erosion and **uplift** that some batholiths become exposed at the surface. Uplift can occur for a variety of reasons. After a continental glacier melts away, the land rebounds and rises. Batholiths are also formed when there is a movement of the crust along **fault zones** where segments may ride up higher than others. As well, there could be tectonic **deformation** (crumpling of the crust), which can cause some parts of the Earth to rise. When there is a collision of two crustal plates, one edge is bound to rise. If one edge is a continental crust and the other is oceanic, it is the continental crust that will rise due to its lower specific gravity (density). Even severe erosion in a region can cause uplift.

Magma is a hot liquid that moves through the Earth's crust, sometimes following fractures and sometimes collecting in a reservoir, called a chamber. While the magma is still molten (liquefied by heat), early-formed crystals may settle to the bottom of the chamber, creating layers in the batholith. The composition of the remaining magma will change with the removal of these crystals. Usually, the cooling magma rises up through the crust towards the surface and, due to this, the solidified crystals rise through the liquid and thus are removed from the magma chamber. The magma chamber is a reservoir that stays fixed 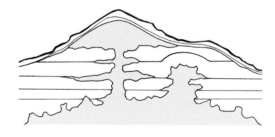 in one area while the crystals travel by natural buoyancy (density differences) and are carried by flow mechanisms. As some minerals leave the magma chamber, the remaining liquid evolves and changes in composition.

All rock bodies formed in the Earth's crust are called intrusions. Along the top of the batholith all large knobs are called **stocks** (small intrusions). Small **domes** protruding from the top of a batholith are named cupolas. A **dike** is a type of igneous intrusive rock that cuts across rocks from an earlier geologic period. **Country rocks** are the bedrock of the region, and existed before the magma collected in the chamber. A series of dikes, all formed from the same magma source at about the same time, constitute a **dike swarm**. A tabular sheet of igneous rock that intrudes between, and is parallel to, the existing rock layers is called a **sill**. In both dikes and **sills**, the rock near the edges is normally very fine-grained because the magma chills rapidly, and minerals form, then harden into an interlocking solid. The magma in the centre of the dike or sill has had more time to cool down and the resulting minerals have a longer time to grow; therefore, the centre will have some coarser-grained crystals.

A pegmatite is an interesting rock type for mineral collectors. Pegmatites are formed in parts of a magma chamber, which are rich in liquids, gases, and some unusual elements. Whether these magmas crystallize in place or move into dikes, these rocks usually develop very coarse-grained crystals. Individual mineral crystals 30 metres in length can sometimes be found. Because pegmatites are formed from rare elements, some unusual minerals can be found.

Volcanic (Extrusive) Environments

The **feeder zone** (the area in the crust through which magma travels en route to eruption in a volcano) can be a **vent** (a nearly vertical hole in a volcano), or it may be a line of fractures through the crust. A **lava flow** is a body of rock formed by a single outpouring of lava through the feeder zone. In addition to lava, **ash**, gases, and wall rock fragments are also expelled from volcanoes. The ejected material trickles back down around the vent, along with the lava that flows on the surface, and eventually, over a period of time, a cone-shaped mass, the volcano, is formed. A **pipe** is a vertical, cylindrical mass of rock, formed in what was the vent of a volcano. A pipe will normally form towards the end of volcanic activity.

With a long-lived magma chamber under a volcano, certain elements will become depleted as eruptions continue, which means that the composition of the lava will change over time. A common rock produced from lava is basalt, which commonly forms ropelike textures. If, for example, lava flows underwater, distinctive pillow shapes are created due to a glassy skin that forms with the very rapid chilling of the outer surface. The pillows are separate bundles of magma, which will continue to roll down the underwater slope until they accumulate in a basin. The interior of the pillow will cool down and thus a solid mass of rock will be formed.

All debris blasted into the air by a volcano is called **pyroclastic** material. Great layers of ash may accumulate and solidify to form a layered rock. A **bomb** is a chunk of lava that solidifies as it flies through the air and these bombs can sometimes be found in ash deposits.

In some places, lava pours out along long fissures or cracks in the Earth's surface. A runny basalt lava moves rapidly away from the fissure, flowing downslope, and forming no volcanic cone. The largest rock masses in the world are a result of these flood basalts. Fissures develop where the continental crust is rifted (pulled apart so that the crust fractures). If a suitable magma chamber is located nearby, then the magma will travel along this new path, up the new fractures to the surface.

Igneous Rocks in Nunavut

Igneous rocks are common all over Nunavut. One of the most famous bodies, clearly visible from an airplane, is the huge Muskox intrusion south of Kugluktuk. It consists of a feeder dike, distinct sides, a roof to the chamber, and, within the magma chamber, a layered series of gabbro and pyroxenite. The layers were formed from the different minerals that crystallized early on, as opposed to those that crystallized later. Farther north, the Coppermine River basalts are an example of vast flood basalts, which are related to this Muskox intrusion. The term flood is used to indicate how vast these flows of lava were.

In Rankin Inlet, the green rocks exposed around the oil tank farm are pillowed basalts from an ancient volcano. The pillows are now oval-shaped and flattened, indicating that after they solidified there was a deformation event that compressed the rocks. Gas bubbles (some empty and some filled with minerals) can be seen in a few locations.

At the northwest end of Baffin Island, there are several bodies of kimberlite. This is a type of volcanic rock that was formed in a relatively short-lived but very explosive event. The magma originated in the Earth's mantle (thick layer of the Earth between the crust and the core). Geologists know a volcano created these kimberlite bodies because they found minerals that are only stable at the ultra-high pressures and temperatures of mantle levels. The kimberlite magma moved with great force up through the crust, ripping away chunks of the surrounding country rocks. After the eruption, unusual minerals and rock fragments settled around the vent, and eventually solidified to form kimberlite. Not only can geologists learn about the mantle from these unique minerals, but the kimberlites do, on occasion, host diamonds.

Part Thirteen

Sedimentary Rock Settings

Detrital Environments

Tiny particles of rock (called sediment) can be carried by wind, water, and ice. Sediment moves from the outcrop (bedrock that sticks up through the overlying cover of glacial debris) where it originated, to a new site of deposition.

Lithification is the process through which a recently deposited sediment is converted into a hardened rock.

Diagenesis is a process that happens when an accumulation of tiny rock particles bury older sediments. Near the Earth's surface, the process of diagenesis happens at low temperatures. This causes pressure to form, and any water present to be pushed out, so that the rock particles become compacted. Some welding of particles may occur. This is one way that sedimentary rocks are formed. A similar process occurs when **cementation** takes place. Cementation happens when new minerals crystallize out of the water that sits around tiny particles of rock. As the new minerals crystallize, they interlock and form a tight solid that also traps the grains or rocks in the surrounding area until a new solid rock has formed.

Detrital particles (gravel, sand, silt, or any other material produced by erosion) may be dropped by wind, water, or ice in a wide variety of environments. An **alluvial fan** (deposit of clay, silt, sand, and gravel) forms where sediments reach a wider section of a river, usually at the base of a confined valley or canyon. Glaciers often have an outwash fan, formed when a meltwater river dumps its load of gravel beyond the edge of the ice.

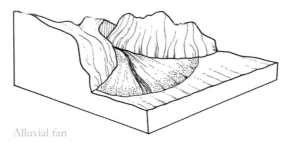

Alluvial fan

Fluvial plains are located beside rivers and are formed when rivers overflow. Sandy deserts commonly exhibit dunes that are made of fine sand. These sand particles are termed **aeolian** deposits, since they are transported and shaped by the wind.

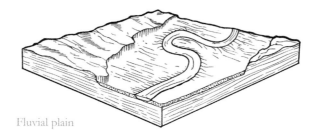

Fluvial plain

Deltas are found in coastal environments where a large river dumps out into a large lake or sea. This environment is very complex due to the great number of physical controls on sedimentation such as wind strength and consistency, or flow rate and direction of water. Besides the abundant detrital sediments laid down in deltas, the formation of **petroleum**- and **gas**-bearing rocks, as well as coal layers, may also occur. In deeper waters off the edge of the oceanic **shelf**, detrital sediments are found on the slope and in the deep basins.

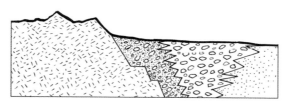

Delta

Biogenic Environments

Biogenic (organic) sediments form on a carbonate shelf, a shallow water shelf, located next to a landmass. Shallow water and sunlight are of critical importance, as these are the features that allow carbonate-producing organisms (clams, mollusca, corals, etc.) to thrive. Once carbonate sediments begin to accumulate, the shallow water must be maintained through the **subsidence** (gradual caving in or sinking) of the shelf area, in order for thick accumulations of sediments to form.

When shells of animals, such as mollusca and bivalves, accumulate in a significant way, a fossil limestone will be formed. Coral reefs may become buried in sand and silt and will then eventually form a coral limestone.

Chert can also form from the silica-rich skeletons of sea creatures called **radiolaria**. These skeletons rain down through the seawater to the ocean floor and eventually a very hard rock will be formed.

Chemical Environments

Chemical sediments are formed from an oversaturation of elements in water. In situations where the outlet to a lake or sea is blocked and all the water evaporates, certain chemical elements become supersaturated in the water and precipitate out of solution, forming rock layers. Vast deposits of salt, gypsum, and potash are created in this way.

Near **oceanic ridges**, there are supersaturated silica waters that may collect in restricted basins and form chert. In lagoon environments, calcium carbonate crystallizes, falls to the sea floor, and accumulates as limestone. If steady tides, currents, and waves agitate this lagoon, calcium carbonate builds up in **concentric** layers around specks of silica, forming little balls called **oolites**. When these oolites are cemented together, they form oolitic limestone.

Sedimentary Rocks in Nunavut

Many types of sedimentary rocks are found across Nunavut. From Cambridge Bay, Victoria Island, past Resolute, and on to Arctic Bay, there are vast deposits of limestone and shale. Of particular interest are occurrences of highly valuable minerals like sphalerite, galena, and pyrite, some of which were so rich that they were mined at the Polaris and Nanisivik mines.

Fuel deposits are formed from the remains of plants and animals. Scientists have determined that the Sverdrup Basin, rich in fuel deposits, was a tropical environment some 65 to 50 million years ago, thriving with activity and plant life. Now, in the Sverdrup Basin around Axel Heiberg Island, a huge marine basin is host to detrital sediments and carbonate deposition. These sedimentary rocks host oil and gas deposits, as well as extensive coal layers.

Just northwest of Rankin Inlet is an interesting area for sedimentary rocks, which are truly ancient. These are translucents, or dirty sandstones formed along the edge of a marine slope. Associated with translucents are greywacke, sandstone, and a chemical sediment called iron formation. Iron formation often contains metallic minerals, and at Meliadine Lake this rock also contains large quantities of gold.

Part Fourteen

Metamorphic Rock Settings

Static Metamorphism

Static metamorphism is a type of solid-to-solid change. Rock masses at or near the surface will sink deeper into the crust when a large mass of sediments is deposited over them. In a mountain valley, for example, if many avalanches occur, the **blocks** will pile up and can exert a downward force. The temperature of the descending rocks rises due to the **geothermal gradient**. Along with a temperature increase, there is a pressure rise, a product of the weight of the rocks pressing down. As the sinking rocks are exposed to rises in both temperature and pressure, they change from one rock type to another.

Regional Metamorphism

The Earth's crust is relatively thin and floats on a layer of the mantle, which is liquid. Therefore, plates of continental crust can collide, fold, fracture, deflect, and even overlap. This is called **plate tectonics**. This metamorphism differs from static metamorphism in that it involves some **tangential** pressures instead of just a downward force. This second type of solid-to-solid transformation is called regional metamorphism. These tangential pressures push and pull from different directions. Large-scale movements of continents, for example, are a cause of regional metamorphism.

Regionally **metamorphosed** rocks have textures, which indicate the directional forces that changed them; thus these rocks usually display a general flattening of the minerals. Any new minerals that crystallize are generally much more **platy** (shaped like a plate) than the original minerals.

As forces increase in a region of rock, **anhydrous** (completely without water) minerals, which are not platy, will form. One example is potassic feldspar, a tabular (long and wide but quite thin, like a table) mineral. This feldspar gives a very dense texture to the rock. Eye-shaped **pods** of potassic feldspar will occur in a gneiss (pronounced "nice"), a rock with segregated light- and dark-coloured layers.

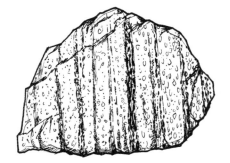

Gneiss

If forces continue to increase in the presence of some water, this potassic feldspar will melt again, producing a little sweat with a granite composition. This new magma (hot fluid) will travel through the parent rock a short distance, then crystallize and solidify into little **veins**, folded layers, and **nodules** (small lumps, distinct from their surroundings). The resulting rock is a migmatite. If this process continues with even higher pressure and temperature, there will be enough moving magma to create a new igneous rock once it solidifies.

Contact Metamorphism

This type of change is also called thermal metamorphism due to the heat given off by a new intrusion of magma in the area. An intrusion is a body of magma that collects in one spot in the Earth's crust and slowly cools to form a solid rock body. A new intrusion will heat up the surrounding country rocks (basic geological formations underlying a region), whether they are igneous, sedimentary, or pre-existing metamorphic rocks. Fluids and **volatiles** (gases) in the **contact zone** tend to be pushed away from the intrusion. High temperature and pressure minerals are formed in this way and large crystals can form due to the long-term circulation of hot gases and fluids that carry elements needed for crystal growth. Hornfels are common metamorphic rocks (usually spotted) found in the contact zone (area surrounding the intrusion).

Cataclastic Metamorphism

Cataclastic metamorphism happens on a smaller scale than the previously described types of metamorphism. As two rock masses move past one another, along a fault zone, for example, they grind against each other and a system of fractures develops. With friction there is heat generation and, if sufficient re-melting happens, a mylonite is formed. A mylonite is a rock in which most original textures are smeared and only tiny remnants of original grains are scattered through the rock.

Impact Metamorphism

The force of a meteorite striking the Earth causes impact metamorphism. **Shock waves** travel through the rock at the impact site, imparting great energy to the rocks. Some rare minerals may be formed under these unusual circumstances. Impact metamorphism is the most common type of metamorphism on the moon.

Around Iqaluit, on southern Baffin Island, a large region of rock called granodiorite gneiss was created by regional metamorphism. These striped black-and-pink rocks are very tough and form the rugged landscape. Further south, around Kimmirut and Cape Dorset, limestone has been regionally metamorphosed to form marble. Contact metamorphism occurred in several places in these marbles, creating a rock called skarn. Inuit prospectors discovered the potentially valuable mineral sapphire in the skarn.

On the north end of Baffin Island and west to the Melville Peninsula, migmatitic gneisses are found over large areas. These rocks have the mineralogical composition of granodiorite and quartz monzonite, but are very metamorphosed. A particularly special place in Nunavut is Marble Island, 32 kilometres south of Rankin Inlet.

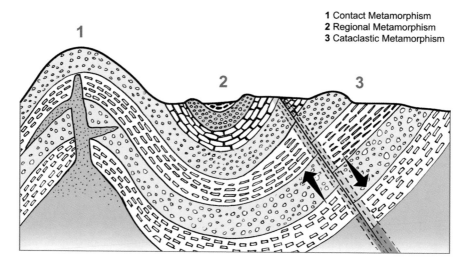

1 Contact Metamorphism
2 Regional Metamorphism
3 Cataclastic Metamorphism

Early visitors to this impressive rock should have named it Quartzite Island, because it is made of quartz, not marble. This island is made of metamorphosed sandstone that is so fine and white it looks like snow. The rocks at Marble Island have a superficial resemblance to marble and even display a wiggly fracture pattern common in marble, but the mineral constituents of this rock are quartz crystals, making it a quartzite.

Most of the rocks in Nunavut are truly ancient. They are among the oldest in the world, because there has been plenty of time for metamorphism, of one type or another, to occur. Metamorphic rocks can be found in most places. Happy hunting!

Part Fifteen

Geologic Time Scale

Most scientists agree that the earth was created 4.6 billion years ago and that it has undergone great changes since then. By examining the rocks exposed at the surface, geologists find many clues that lead to a better understanding of the history of our planet.

There are four fundamental principles that help us to decide a rock's age.

First, there is the principle of superposition, which states that in any undeformed sequence of rock layers, the oldest layer is found at the bottom. Successively younger layers lay above it.

The principle of original horizontality relies on the fact that detrital sediments sink in a fluid under the influence of gravity (a force that pulls an object towards the centre of the earth), therefore rock layers are initially horizontal. Angled layers of sedimentary rock indicate that those rocks have been disturbed by folding and faulting (when two blocks of crust move on either side of a large **fault**).

The principle of cross-cutting relationships states that when magma crystallizes within the Earth's crust, forming an igneous intrusion, this body must be younger than the rocks that surround it.

When there is a break in the rock sequence as a result of erosion or because sediments were no longer being deposited in an area, the principle of unconformity comes into play. The layers on either side of the angular unconformity are easy to spot since the older strata are cut off by the younger strata, and the two sets of layers are at different angles to one another.

Trilobite fossil   Photo: Shutterstone.com

Geologists use these principles to devise a geologic column (chart for an area). Once several columns are determined across a region, then the overall pattern of rock deposition and intrusion can be evaluated.

In a geologic column, the oldest rocks are placed at the bottom of the chart and the younger rocks just above it. Fossils are used to help determine the age of rocks. Fossils are the casts and tracks of plants and animals preserved in the rocks. A cast is formed when a soft substance gradually hardens around an object and makes a permanent mold of the item, like when a cast is placed over a broken leg. Index fossils occurred in a relatively short period of the Earth's history, but are widespread. Index fossils are particularly useful for determining the relative age of rocks and for allowing scientists to link together geologic columns from widely scattered places. Marine index fossils are rocks that were once under an ancient sea.

To calculate the precise age of a rock, measurements are taken of how much **isotope** is present compared to how much daughter element exists—this is called **radiometric dating**. When the centre of the atoms in the element has the same number of protons but a differing number of neutrons, this is called an isotope. For example, Carbon-12

Photo: Mélanie Houde

and Carbon-14 are both isotopes of carbon, one with six neutrons and one with eight neutrons (both with six protons). Some isotopes are more stable than others. Particles can be lost from the **nucleus** (centre) to create a stable daughter element. For example, Uranium-238 will convert to lead at a steady and predictable rate. In 4.5 billion years, half of the total amount of U238 converts to lead. This is considered to be the isotope's half-life.

Through the understanding of these principles and radiometric dating, scientists have been able to devise a geologic column for Nunavut. Four main age divisions are recognized: the Slave province, the Churchill province, the Bear province, and the Arctic Platform.

The Slave province exposes Archean age rocks (older than 2.5 billion years) that were formed on a stable **continental plate**, found in the Kitikmeot region. The rocks are mainly volcanic and intrusive (formed inside the Earth's crust), with sandstones, shales, and gneisses. Just across the border in the Northwest Territories, the oldest rocks in the world are found in the Slave. They are the Acasta Gneiss and are dated at four billion years old.

The Churchill province is found in the Kivalliq region and has rocks of Archean to Proterozoic age (from 1.8 billion to 600 million years old). These rocks are mostly volcanic, intrusive, and sedimentary.

The Bear province, of the Proterozoic age, occurs in the Coronation Gulf and Victoria Island areas. These rocks were formed on an ancient **continental plate**, which then collided with the older Slave **craton** (large stable block of the Earth's crust forming the nucleus of a continent).

During the early Paleozoic time (around 550 to 600 million years ago), the centre of the continent was lower than it is now and was covered by warm, shallow seas. Thick sedimentary sequences (related groups of layers) were laid down. These rocks are well exposed in the High Arctic (Qikiqtani region) and include sandstones, shales, limestones, dolostones, and minor volcanic rocks. This area is called the Arctic Platform. A collision of two slowly moving crustal plates occurred during the late Silurian and the early Tertiary periods (420 and 50 million years ago, respectively), which led to the creation of the mountains of eastern Baffin Island and the High Arctic.

Mineral Descriptions

Diamond

Native Element – Diamond – C
Alternate Names: Bort; carbonado
Family and Crystal System: Native element; cubic (three **axes** of equal lengths, all perpendicular to one another)

Appearance

Diamond is commonly found in **crystal** form and resembles two pyramids joined at the base (eight-sided **octahedron**). Generally colourless to yellowish, diamonds can also be black or any other colour. Sometimes the faces of the crystal are curved, and **twinning** is also common.

Crystals are transparent to **translucent** and their **lustre** makes them look like hard minerals. The brilliant shine of this mineral is unique and is called **adamantine**. When looking into a clear-cut stone, a distinct fire is discernible and this occurs because the rays of light bend in many directions within the cut stone.

Physical Properties

Diamond is most famous for being the hardest known substance. On the **Mohs scale** of hardness (the relative ease of being scratched) from 1 to 10, diamond ranks 10. However, even though diamond is very hard, it is still **brittle** and can shatter if struck sharply. The **specific gravity** of diamond is 3.5, and diamond also displays a **perfect cleavage**, which means that when the stone breaks, it breaks off along new faces parallel to the eight original faces. This mineral is often fluorescent, giving off light of its own when lit by an ultraviolet light.

Environment & Occurrence

Diamond can only form under high pressure and temperature conditions. In the upper **mantle**, diamonds form in a rock called kimberlite, which rises very rapidly through the Earth's **crust** and erupts explosively at the surface. When these kimberlite rocks erode, the diamonds can be concentrated in the loose sand that weathers away from the kimberlite. This is where most natural diamonds are found.

Canada has become the third greatest producer of gem-quality diamonds in the world.

One of Canada's top diamond producers is the Jericho diamond mine in Nunavut, which opened in 2006. This mine is about 350 kilometres southwest of Cambridge Bay and is expected to have a mine life of nine years. In the meantime, the owners continue to explore nearby for other kimberlites, hoping to find another site as rich in diamond.

Did You Know?

Photo: Royal Ontario Museum

The name for this mineral comes from a twisted version of *adamas*, the Greek word meaning invincible. Diamond was given this name because of its **hardness**. Bort is the name given to industrial grade diamonds that are used for saw blades, abrasives, and other grinding apparatus, while carbonado is the name given to extremely fine-grained diamonds that can only be seen under a microscope.

Diamond is highly valued as a gemstone for jewellery due to its hardness and its fire. It is the most common stone chosen for engagement rings. A gem-cutter working with diamond will calculate the best angle at which to cut the **facets** to maximize the amount of light that bounces around and behind the top of the stone. The more the light returns to the top surface, the more brilliant the appearance.

Native Elements

Graphite

Native Element – Graphite – C
Alternate Names: Plumbago
Family and Crystal System: Native element; **hexagonal** (three out of four **axes** lie on the same plane, are of equal lengths, and intersect at 120°; fourth axis is not the same length and not perpendicular)

Appearance

Graphite **crystals** are rare. Graphite usually occurs as sheetlike, scaly, or **granular** masses. A good crystal is a simple **tabular** form. The colour is dark grey to black and so is the **streak** (the powder left on a piece of porcelain when a mineral is dragged across it). Graphite has a metallic **lustre** and is **opaque**.

Physical Properties

Graphite breaks easily into perfect flat sheets (it has **good cleavage**) and the resulting flakes are flexible, but inelastic. The flakes bend, but they break instead of bending back. The grains are very soft, measuring 1 on the **Mohs scale**. The **specific gravity** is 2.2, which makes this a very light mineral. Graphite has a distinctly greasy feel and will leave fingers black.

Photo: Royal Ontario Museum

Environment & Occurrence

Graphite is a common mineral and occurs in a wide variety of geologic environments. It is widespread in coal **deposits**, limestone, schist, and gneiss. Small amounts may be found in igneous rocks, pegmatites, and in **veins**.

In the mineral-rich Kimmirut area, graphite occurs widely in the marbles and in the calc-silicate skarn—the host rock to the sapphire mineral **occurrence**. A graphite schist is a significant rock type in the area.

The name graphite results from the Greek word *graphein*—to write. In ancient times graphite was used as an implement for drawing and writing, which is why graphite is the lead in your pencil.

The mineral formula for diamond is exactly the same as the formula for graphite. The two minerals have very different molecular structures, though, which explains why diamond is the hardest mineral known to man, and graphite is almost the softest.

Graphite is used in industry for casting and melting applications, because it holds up well under ultra-high temperatures. It is an excellent conductor of electricity, which is why graphite is used to manufacture electrodes. But golfers and fishers should get out of a thunderstorm (their clubs and rods are made out of graphite) to avoid being struck by lightning!

Graphite makes a great lubricant and is also included as a dye in some paints. The purest graphite is used in nuclear reactors to shield the nuclear fission process and make it safe.

Photo: Danny Christopher

Native Elements

Silver

Native Element – Silver – Ag
Alternate Names: Native silver
Family and Crystal System: Native element; cubic (three axes of equal lengths, all perpendicular to one another)

Appearance

Silver generally occurs in masses, **tabular** shapes, and scaly groups. Good **crystals** of silver are very rare. Silver can also form **nuggets**. On rare occasions it is found in wiry clusters, some of which resemble branches from a plant. The colour of this mineral is silvery white, but when it is tarnished it changes to grey or black on the surface. Silver is **opaque** and shiny, and has a metallic **lustre**.

Physical Properties

Silver is malleable, which means it can be hammered or bent into various shapes without breaking or cracking. It does not have **cleavage** (the way a mineral breaks along well-defined planes of weakness). If fractured, it exhibits a **hackly** fracture, which is very spiky. Silver is quite soft, registering a 2.5 to 3 on the **Mohs scale**. One of the key properties of silver is that it is quite heavy. It has a **specific gravity** of 10. If a bit of silver is scratched across unglazed porcelain it will leave a **streak** that is silvery white to light lead grey.

Environment & Occurrence

Native silver is generally found in **veins, deposited** there by hot fluids that circulate through the ground. Besides water, these fluids also carry many other elements, such as silica, calcium, fluorine, gold, silver, zinc, iron, copper, and many other metal ions. When the fluid starts to cool down over time, it cannot continue to carry all the elements, and so crystals of various minerals form from those elements. Silver is one of the minerals found in this sort of vein.

Small quantities of silver often occur in native gold. One locality with a great abundance of silver is the Hackett River project, just south of Bathurst Inlet in the Kitikmeot region. Most rocks at this location are rhyolite tuff. Within these rocks are veinlets (small **veins**) and **massive** bodies of copper, zinc, silver, and gold. Silver is the richest mineral found at this location.

Did You Know?

Silver is widely used to make jewellery and is also used in the photographic emulsion needed to capture an image on film. Silver is also used in the manufacturing of electrical components (it is the best known conductor of heat and electricity), cutlery, coins, and tableware.

Four thousand years ago, a very rich silver mine in Bohemia produced silver coins called *Joachimsthaler*. Later the name of these coins became shortened to *thaler* and eventually formed the word dollar that we use today.

Photo: Royal Ontario Museum

Native Elements

Arsenopyrite

Sulphide – Arsenopyrite – FeAsS
Alternate Names: Mispickel
Family and Crystal System: Sulphide; monoclinic (three **axes** all of different lengths; two axes perpendicular; third axis inclined)

Appearance

Prismatic crystals of arsenopyrite are common. **Twinning** is also common. Arsenopyrite may also be found in **granular** form and compact masses. The colour is typically silvery white to steel grey and the **streak** is black. Arsenopyrite has a metallic **lustre** and is **opaque**. It may take on a brown **tarnish**.

Photo: Royal Ontario Museum

Physical Properties

Arsenopyrite has one distinct and one **indistinct cleavage**. On the **Mohs scale**, arsenopyrite registers at 5.5 to 6, and it has a **specific gravity** of 6.1, which makes it a heavy mineral. If an arsenopyrite specimen is heated or struck by a hard object, it gives off a distinct garlic smell. Arsenopyrite has an uneven fracture pattern.

Environment & Occurrence

Arsenopyrite is found in **veins** formed by hot fluids continually circulating through the rock, known as hydrothermal fluids. It can usually be found with gold in quartz veins. In a **contact metamorphic** setting (rocks that are changed because of heat from a hot **magma** body), arsenopyrite occurs with scheelite. Arsenopyrite may also occur in pegmatites.

Arsenopyrite sometimes contains tiny grains of gold, and it may be mined for its gold content.

At the former Lupin gold mine, in the Kitikmeot region, arsenopyrite occurred next to quartz veins. The veins and arsenopyrite were hosted in an iron formation, a banded **sedimentary** which contains many iron-rich minerals. Found along with the arsenopyrite were pyrrhotite, pyrite, loellingite, and gold.

Did You Know?

Arsenopyrite contains arsenic and is sometimes mined for this resource. Arsenic goes into the production of herbicides and insecticides, as well as medicines.

Sulphides

Chalcopyrite

Sulphide – Chalcopyrite – CuFeS$_2$
Family and Crystal System: Sulphide; tetragonal (the **crystals** are more elongated than a cube; three **axes** all perpendicular to one another; two of the axes are the same lengths, while the main axis is a different length)

Appearance

Chalcopyrite is generally found in **massive** form, thus crystals are rarely seen. Occasionally a good crystal is found. A good crystal can be characterized as a **sphenoid** shape. Sometimes **twinning** can be observed. **Striations** may sometimes be observed on the faces.

Chalcopyrite is brassy yellow, sometimes with a green tinge, and has a metallic **lustre**. It can **tarnish** to an iridescent rainbow of colours, much like a peacock's tail, so some people refer to it as a peacock tarnish. Chalcopyrite is classified as **opaque**. If a chalcopyrite grain is fractured, it will reveal an uneven surface, with no particular pattern. The **streak** is greenish black.

Physical Properties

Chalcopyrite lacks a **distinct cleavage**, which means it is not likely to have well-developed breaks along well-defined planes of weakness. It is **brittle**. On the **Mohs scale**, chalcopyrite has a **hardness** of 3.5 to 4, and its **specific gravity** is 4.2, which makes it heavier than most minerals.

Environment & Occurrence

This mineral occurs in a wide variety of rock types. It can be found in most types of igneous rocks and in **contact metamorphic** rock. Chalcopyrite is also found in some **sedimentary** rocks, such as slate.

Chalcopyrite is the most widespread copper mineral in the world and is mined in many environments.

Chalcopyrite can occur in tiny grains spread evenly through the igneous rocks, or

Photo: Royal Ontario Museum

it can occur in more concentrated **lenses** and **veins**. A vein forms when a mineral (or minerals) **crystallizes** in a pre-existing crack in the rock. Calcopyrite, or copper porphyry systems, make up some of the largest examples of metallic **mineralization** in the world. Mineralization describes an unusually large abundance of a particular mineral in one locality. If the mineral in question is highly valuable, then a geologist will want to determine whether the mineral is economic to mine. Many factors must be considered in evaluating the economics of a mine. For example, if it is determined that the mineral can be extracted for a profit, the geologist can then refer to that mass of mineral as a mineral **deposit**.

A porphyry system is a region of the Earth's **crust** located above an **igneous intrusion**, full of **fractures** through which a hot fluid circulates. As the fluid gradually moves away from the hot intrusion, the fluid cools and can no longer hold some of the

Sulphides

metals it carries in solution, causing the metals to dissolve into a liquid form. As the temperature drops, the substance will eventually take on its solid form again. Crystals will form in the veinlets and fractures. This is how **veins** are created.

The High Lake project is situated just south of Coronation Gulf. Exploration efforts there have outlined several large copper, zinc, gold, and silver deposits. The copper occurs as chalcopyrite and the deposits average about 5% copper. The High Lake deposits are among the richest undeveloped copper **occurrences** in the world.

Photo: Danny Christopher

Did You Know?

Copper is a very important metal, so chalcopyrite, as a source of copper, is often mined. Copper is used for electrical wiring, water pipes and fittings, bronze, brass, and other **alloys**. Copper is also used for roofing material.

Due to its brassy yellow colour, chalcopyrite is often mistaken for gold. However, gold is much heavier and softer, is not **brittle**, and never tarnishes.

Sulphides

Galena

Sulphide – Galena – PbS
Family and Crystal System: Sulphide; cubic (three **axes** of equal lengths, all perpendicular to one another)

Appearance

Crystals are common and generally look like square boxes. Sometimes the corners of the boxes are lopped off. Galena can exhibit **striations** that run on the diagonal, which resemble a series of scratches or fine parallel lines. When the grain size is smaller, galena can form coarse to fine **granular** masses, like piles of salt. Galena is a metallic mineral, therefore it is **opaque**. Light reflects off the surfaces with a metallic **lustre**. The colour of the mineral and its **streak** is lead grey, with a slight reddish tint. Twinned crystals can occur.

Photo: Danny Christopher

Physical Properties

Galena exhibits a **perfect cleavage** that is parallel to the boxlike sides. It has a tendency to break into small cubes. This mineral is just 2.5 on the **Mohs scale**, but its **specific gravity** is 7.6. Galena has a **brittle** fracture.

Environment & Occurrence

Galena is the most important lead-bearing mineral. It is associated with a few types of silver-bearing minerals and can contain silver **inclusions** in quantities rich enough to mine. Galena is quite common and is found in **veins** with other sulphide minerals. Veins and cavities in limestone often have galena with sphalerite, a zinc-rich mineral. Galena is found in rocks affected by **contact metamorphism**. Sometimes it is also found disseminated through **sediments**.

At the now-closed Polaris mine north of Resolute, galena was medium- to coarse-grained and associated with banded sphalerite (a zinc sulphide). Both the galena and the banded sphalerite occurred in limestone.

Did You Know?

Lead is used extensively in electric batteries and ammunition. It can also be found in cables, pipes, lead glass, and radiation protection.

Photo: Royal Ontario Museum

Sulphides

Pyrite

Sulphide – Pyrite – FeS$_2$
Alternate Names: Fool's gold
Family and Crystal System: Sulphide; cubic (three **axes** of equal lengths, all perpendicular to one another)

Appearance

Pyrite will commonly form cube-shaped **crystals** or eight-sided double pyramids, called **octahedrons**. Many variations of these two shapes are also found. The sides of the cube often have **striations**. **Twins** are common. Pyrite will also form in **massive**, **granular**, **radiating** (oriented like spokes in a wheel), globular, or stalactitic forms. **Stalactites** form in cave environments where waters drip steadily over the same spot and create pointy growths of minerals.

Pyrite is a distinctive brass yellow colour and has a greenish black **streak**. Pyrite is always **opaque**, as no light can pass through it. It has a metallic **lustre**.

Physical Properties

Pyrite has a **conchoidal** fracture, which means the fractured surface will be curved like a clamshell. It is also **brittle** and will easily break into small chunks. No **cleavage** is observed and so it does not break into regular, flat planes. Its **hardness** on the **Mohs scale** is 6 to 6.5. Pyrite is fairly heavy, with a measurement of 5 as its **specific gravity**.

When pyrite is exposed to the atmosphere, as at the Earth's surface, it tends to rust. Orange to yellow staining of **bedrock** exposures is often a sign that pyrite is in the vicinity. Once this staining occurs, the mineral is called limonite.

Photo: Danny Christopher

Photo: Dante Christopher

Environment & Occurrence

Not only is pyrite a common mineral, it is the most common sulphide mineral, and can be found in almost every geological environment. In **igneous** rocks, however, pyrite is found in very small amounts. In **sedimentary** rocks such as chalk beds (layers), pyrite may form **concretions**. Concretions grow from the centre outwards, around a central point or **nucleus**, forming balls. Pyrite is also commonly found in coal beds. An abundance of pyrite exists in **hydrothermal vein deposits**, which are formed by the continual circulation of hot fluids. These veins contain various metals and elements within a rock's fractures. Eventually crystals grow in these vein settings, among them pyrite.

World-class pyrite specimens were commonplace at the Nanisivik mine, near Arctic Bay. An incredible diversity of crystal forms were discovered at the mine, making it a mineral collector's heaven. One of the reasons for this huge variety in form is that the pyrite replaced another mineral called marcasite. Replacement can be caused by changes in temperature, excessive heat, or changes in fluids in the area. Marcasite has the same formula as pyrite, but it has a different molecular structure and is **orthorhombic**, not cubic, like pyrite. Orthorhombic minerals tend to be rectangular and bladed, or else **tabular**. Marcasite can also form a **cockscomb aggregate**, which looks like a fan of spear shaped segments. Since the pyrite replaced marcasite at this location, the change in composition has resulted in many unusual shapes.

Sulphides

Photo: Royal Ontario Museum

The name pyrite is from the Greek word *pyr*, which means fire. This choice of name arose from the fact that pyrite will create sparks when struck against steel.

Although pyrite contains iron, there is not enough to make this an important source of iron for industry. It is mined, though, for the manufacture of sulphuric acid and iron sulphates, which are both very useful chemicals.

At times, pyrite will contain some gold or copper within its molecular structure (hidden inside the specimen). Thus pyrite is occasionally mined for the gold and copper it contains.

The name fool's gold was given to pyrite because many people mistakenly thought they had found gold when, in fact, they had found pyrite. Gold is softer, not **brittle**, and a much warmer, richer mustard yellow colour.

Sulphides

Pyrrhotite

Sulphide – Pyrrhotite – Fe$_{1-x}$S
Alternate Names: Pyrrhotine
Family and Crystal System: Sulphide; monoclinic (three **axes** all of different lengths; two axes perpendicular; third axis is inclined) or **hexagonal** (three out of four axes lie on the same plane, are of equal lengths, and intersect at 120°; fourth axis not the same length and not perpendicular)

Appearance

Pyrrhotite **crystals** are rare and mostly **massive** and **granular**. Rare crystals are **tabular**.

Pyrrhotite is a dull greyish yellow, bronzy yellow, coppery bronze red, or brown colour. It may tarnish to a dark brown. Pyrrhotite has a metallic **lustre** and is **opaque**. If scratched against a piece of unglazed porcelain, the **streak** is greyish black.

Physical Properties

The **cleavage** of pyrrhotite is not usually distinct and if it fractures it presents an uneven face. On the **Mohs scale**, the mineral is 3.5 to 4.5 and the **specific gravity** is 4.6, which makes it a fairly heavy mineral. Pyrrhotite is a **magnetic** mineral, but the intensity of its magnetism varies.

Environment & Occurrence

The primary **occurrence** for pyrrhotite is within dark-coloured **igneous** rocks, like gabbro and peridotite. Sometimes large masses of this mineral occur with other sulphide minerals, such as chalcopyrite. Pyrrhotite is also found in **contact metamorphic** rocks and pegmatites. It also is a common mineral in **hydrothermal veins**, where the long-term circulation of hot water has deposited new minerals in pre-existing cracks in rocks.

At Ferguson Lake, which is about 70 kilometres west of Rankin Inlet, fine-grained, disseminated pyrrhotite occurs throughout the gabbro. The iron in the pyrrhotite rusts and gives the rock a rusty orange appearance. This surface feature is called a **gossan**. Gossans can often be seen from aircraft. Chalcopyrite and pentlandite are other minerals found in these gossans.

Pyrrhotite contains iron and has been mined for iron in the past. However, pyrrhotite does not contain as much iron as other minerals, like hematite or magnetite.

Pyrrhotite can contain nickel, cobalt, and platinum and is mined where it occurs in large enough quantities. It is often closely associated with the mineral pentlandite, which also contains nickel.

Photo: Danny Christopher

Photo: Royal Ontario Museum

Sulphides

Sphalerite

Sulphide – Sphalerite – (Zn,Fe²⁺)S
Alternate Names: Blende; zinc blende; black jack
Family and Crystal System: Sulphide; cubic (three **axes** of equal lengths, all perpendicular to one another)

Appearance

Sphalerite **crystals** are common and the typical shape is a three-sided pyramid. Also displayed are complicated crystal forms, as well as all kinds of **twinning**. Sphalerite can also form in a **granular** mass, or be **fibrous**, or **botryoidal**.

Sphalerite can be almost any colour. The zinc-rich variety is mostly yellow or brown, but may also be red, green, white, or colourless. A large amount of iron in the grain makes the mineral almost black. If the mineral is scratched over a porcelain plate, the resulting **streak** is yellow to brown. The **lustre** of sphalerite is also quite variable, ranging from **resinous** to **adamantine** to a greasy metallic shine. The crystals will also range from transparent to **opaque**.

Photo: Royal Ontario Museum

Physical Properties

Sphalerite has a **perfect cleavage** in six directions, thus crystals will break cleanly into smaller minicrystals. Sphalerite is 3.5 to 4 on the **Mohs scale**. The **specific gravity** is 4, which makes it a fairly heavy mineral. If a tiny amount of hydrochloric acid is dropped on the mineral, a rotten egg smell is emitted. Sometimes sphalerite is **fluorescent** and glows brightly under an ultraviolet light.

Environment & Occurrence

Sphalerite is a common mineral and occurs in a wide variety of settings. It is often found with galena. It is very common in rocks affected by **contact metamorphism**. In addition, sphalerite occurs in **hydrothermal veins**, when long-term circulation of hot water has deposited new minerals in pre-existing cracks in rocks.

Just south of Coronation Gulf in the Kitikmeot region is the High Lake zinc **deposit**. Sphalerite is plentiful, along with pyrite, pyrrhotite, chalcopyrite, and galena. The sphalerite there is mostly dark brown, reddish, pale pink white, purplish brown, or even black.

Did You Know?

Sphalerite is mined for the zinc that it contains. Zinc has many uses, including the manufacture of brass and other **alloys**. Sphalerite is used for electroplating and galvanizing iron, batteries, paints, and medicines.

The name sphalerite is derived from a Greek word meaning treacherous. This mineral got its name because it is easily confused with other minerals.

Photo: Danny Christopher

Sulphides

63

Corundum

Oxide – Corundum – Al$_2$O$_3$
Alternate Name: Sapphire; ruby
Family and Crystal System: Oxide; trigonal (three out of four **axes** lie on the same plane, are of equal lengths, and intersect at 120°; fourth axis not the same length and not perpendicular)

Appearance

Corundum **crystals** are the common form for this mineral, and they are barrel-shaped, with steep pyramids at both ends. The faces can be rough and uneven, and may display **striations**. Corundum also occurs in **granular** form; it resembles a pile or layer of small salt grains. The colour is normally grey, a weak blue, yellow, or red, although corundum may be any colour. Crystals display a **vitreous** (glassy) **lustre** and are **translucent** to transparent.

If there are needlelike **inclusions** of other minerals inside the corundum crystal, a star-shaped pattern may be seen.

Physical Properties

Corundum does not have a **cleavage**, which means it does not break into neat and tidy fragments. It is very hard, measuring 9 on the **Mohs scale**. With a **specific gravity** of 4, this mineral is quite heavy. If fractured, a corundum grain displays a **conchoidal** or uneven surface, with no particular pattern.

Environment & Occurrence

Ruby is the red **gemstone** variety of corundum. Sapphire is the name for gem-quality corundum that is blue or any other colour. Small amounts of titanium and iron in the mineral formula cause the corundum to be blue.

Photo: Royal Ontario Museum

Corundum is formed from **igneous** and **metamorphic** rocks. It occurs in some syenites, nepheline syenites, and associated pegmatites. Sometimes it is found along the edges of a peridotite **occurrence**. In metamorphic rocks, look for it in gneiss, mica schist, and marble. As with other very hard minerals, corundum may be found in sands and gravels.

In the Kimmirut area, sapphires that are dark blue with a violet tint, light blue, pink, yellow, and colourless have been discovered. They occur in calc-silicate **pods** in white marble. So far the largest sapphire uncovered measures 20 centimetres. There are at least 15 occurrences of sapphire spread over 4.5 kilometres in the area. A lovely blue cobalt spinel was also discovered along with the sapphires.

Did You Know?

Corundum is mostly used in the manufacture of abrasives (used for grinding or polishing a surface). In nature, corundum may be mixed with magnetite, spinel, and quartz. Together they are called emery and are used as an abrasive.

When crystals are a good size, transparency, and colour, they may be considered gemstones. Fine rubies are among the most sought-after and expensive natural stones in the world and are used to make high-quality jewellery.

Oxides

Hematite

Oxide – Hematite – Fe_2O_3
Alternate Names: Kidney ores; specular hematite
Family and Crystal System: Oxide; trigonal (three out of four **axes** lie on the same plane, are of equal lengths, and intersect at 120°; fourth axis not the same length and not perpendicular)

Appearance

Normally hematite is found in **granular** or earthy masses. It can also occur as scales, rosettes, fibres, radiating fans, kidney-shaped masses, **botryoids**, and in other forms. **Crystals** of hematite are uncommon and when found as flat, **tabular** crystals, they are called specular hematite. Hematite is steely grey to black and may display a blue **iridescence**. Hematite is red when soft and earthy. Scratching a fragment across a piece of unglazed porcelain leaves a dark red, cherry red, or reddish brown **streak**. Hematite is **opaque** and has a metallic **lustre** when coarse-grained and has a flat, matte lustre when fine-grained.

Physical Properties

Hematite does not display **cleavage**. If fractured it has a **conchoidal** pattern. It is a 6 on the **Mohs scale** and it has a **specific gravity** of 5.3, which makes it a fairly heavy mineral. Hematite is not **magnetic**.

Photo: Royal Ontario Museum

Environment & Occurrence

Hematite is fairly common and occurs in several kinds of geological settings. It is the main mineral type found in the world's most important iron **ore deposits**. Hematite is a very desirable mineral found in large enough concentrations to be mined, recovered, and extracted at a profit.

This mineral occurs in **igneous intrusive rocks**, **volcanic** rocks, **contact metamorphic** rocks, and **regional metamorphic** rocks. In **sedimentary** rocks, hematite is most often found in a **banded** iron formation. In this distinctly layered rock, quartz-rich layers alternate with hematite-rich layers. In other sedimentary rocks, red beds result from the rusting of iron minerals to form the red hematite.

On the Mary River, south of Pond Inlet, huge deposits of hematite have been found. This discovery has the potential to become a significant iron mine. Some of the hematite zones are 140 metres wide and, in certain places, specular hematite can be seen.

Photo: Danny Christopher

Did You Know?

The name hematite is derived from the Greek word *aima*, which means blood, due to the similarity of the hematite's streak powder to dried blood. Red ochre is the **massive**, earthy form of hematite. It is used as a polishing powder and a pigment.

Hematite is the main ore of iron, and iron is the key ingredient in the manufacture of steel, cast iron, and various metal **alloys**. Hematite is one of the most important minerals to humans and contributes greatly to man's high standard of living because of its rich ore content.

Oxides

Magnetite

Oxide – Magnetite – $Fe^{2+}Fe^{3+}_2O_4$
Alternate Name: Magnetic iron ore; lodestone
Family and Crystal System: Oxide; spinel group; cubic (three **axes** of equal length, all perpendicular to one another)

Appearance

Good **crystals** are common and generally form what looks like two pyramids joined at their bases. Magnetite also readily forms **granular** masses. The colour is black and so is the **streak** left behind when this mineral is scratched over a piece of porcelain. The metallic shine of the mineral can be dull or bright. Magnetite is **opaque**, which means that light cannot pass through it. Magnetite will also commonly form **twin** crystals, where two crystals seem to be growing out of each other. The place where the two crystals connect is called the **twin plane**.

Photo: Danny Christopher

Physical Properties

The twin plane in twinned magnetite is a plane of weakness and, therefore, the mineral is likely to break along this surface. This property is called **parting** and it is distinct in magnetite. The fracture pattern, when visible, is **conchoidal**. Magnetite is nearly 6 on the **Mohs scale**. The **specific gravity** measures 5.2, which makes it a heavy mineral. The most characteristic property of magnetite is that it is **magnetic**.

Environment & Occurrence

Magnetite is commonly found in many types of **igneous** rocks, where it occurs scattered throughout the rock in very small amounts. Alternatively it may be clumped together in the **magma** (hot fluid in the Earth's **crust** or **mantle**) and then remain a lump once the magma has solidified. Magnetite is one of the Earth's important sources of iron.

In **metamorphic** and **sedimentary** rocks, magnetite can form extensive layers or **lenses**. The associated rocks are called iron formations.

Just south of Pond Inlet, there are enormous magnetite beds along the Mary River. Although they were first discovered in 1962, it is only now that the conditions and price of iron are optimum for mining. Magnetite and hematite occur together in those beds in a very rich form—these hematite **deposits** along the Mary River are possibly among the richest iron deposits in the world.

Due to the natural **weathering** and **erosion** of igneous rocks, magnetite grains can be carried by water and then deposited on a beach along with other light-coloured minerals. Beaches with a lot of magnetite in the sand will be black.

Did You Know?

Magnetite draws the needle of a compass in an area where magnetite is easily found. The needle of the compass will not seek magnetic north; instead, it will pull towards the largest masses of magnetite. So it pays to recognize magnetite when navigating.

Photo: Royal Ontario Museum

Oxides

Spinel

Oxide – Spinel – $MgAl_2O_4$
Alternate Names: Hercynite; gahnite; pleonaste; picotite
Family and Crystal System: Spinel group; cubic (three **axes** of equal lengths, all perpendicular to one another)

Appearance

Spinel **crystals** are common and generally look like two pyramids base to base. **Twins** are also common. It may occur in **granular** or **massive** forms.

Spinel is red when pure, but is also commonly blue, green, brown, black, or purple. Spinel can be colourless, but this is rare. It has a glassy look and allows some or all light to pass through it.

Photo: Royal Ontario Museum

Physical Properties

This is a hard mineral, measuring 7.5 to 8 on the **Mohs scale**. Spinel has a **specific gravity** of 3.6 and so it is a heavy mineral. When the grain fractures, it does so in a **conchoidal** pattern. Spinel does not have a **cleavage**, which means it does not break easily into regular forms.

Environment & Occurrence

Spinels are found in small quantities in dark-coloured **igneous** rocks such as gabbro, in aluminum-rich **metamorphic** rocks, and in limestones affected by **contact metamorphism**. Spinel can sometimes be found in **veins** and pegmatites. Because spinel is such a tough mineral, it is also found as rolled pebbles in sand and gravel.

Near Waddell Bay, on Frobisher Bay, crystals of violet and blue spinel have been found. Grains up to 3 centimetres long have been unearthed and some have very small transparent sections, which are gem-quality. At this location, the spinel sits in calcite grains and is associated with diopside and phlogopite.

Did You Know?

Spinels with great colour and transparency are used as **gemstones**. The name *spinel* is from the Latin, *spina*, which means thorn, and describes how the crystals may be quite spiky.

Oxides

Halite

Halide – Halite – NaCl
Alternate names: Salt; rock salt
Family and Crystal System: Cubic (three **axes** of equal length, all perpendicular to one another)

Appearance

Halite commonly presents good **crystals**, generally as cubes or cubes with stepped faces. Occasionally the faces are concave. This mineral can also occur in **granular** masses. Halite is normally colourless or white, but can be found as yellow, red, brown, purple, or blue crystals. The **lustre** is **vitreous**. Grains are clear or partly so (transparent to **translucent**). Under a **fluorescent** lamp, halite may shine red.

Physical Properties

Good cleavage is evident in three directions and each is parallel to a cube face. Halite is 2 to 2.5 on the **Mohs scale**. It has a 2.2 **specific gravity** and so it is not very heavy. Halite will dissolve in water and has a salty taste. The **streak** is always white, no matter the colour of the crystal. The fracture pattern is uneven or **conchoidal**.

Environment & Occurrence

Halite forms **massive** beds that were once deposited at the bottom of a sea floor. As sea water evaporates, halite is formed. Normally halite layers alternate with layers of gypsum and calcite. These rocks can be referred to as **evaporites**.

If the salt layer is covered by a vast sequence of other **sediments**, the pressure is enough to cause the massive halite to flow like a liquid plastic. Halite will take advantage of cracks in the overlying sediments and squeeze up, forming salt **domes**. Generally, halite is found in rocks that are from the Paleozoic to Recent Age (less than about 600 million years old).

Photo: Danny Christopher

On Axel Heiberg Island, west of Ellesmere Island, researchers have been mapping and learning about approximately 40 salt **domes** that dot the island. Salty spring water flows out of cracks in the ground. The water is very salty because it passes through rising salt domes, dissolving the halite as it moves. Scientists have determined that the salt domes rise about 5 centimetres per year, and that the salt water stays at a steady 6°C year round!

Did You Know?

Halite is widely used by the chemical industry to produce many chemicals that require sodium (Na) and chlorine (Cl). For example, one by-product of halite is soda **ash**, which is required for the manufacture of glass. Halite is also required to make soap. Also, the chlorine constituent found in halite goes into the production of bleach and into water purification systems.

Around the salt domes of Axel Heiberg Island, there is a high potential for finding oil and **gas deposits**. Salt domes are a favoured site for the exploration of oil and gas deposits because the rocks surrounding the salt domes are deformed, creating pockets where **petroleum** can collect. The salt is impervious to petroleum, so the liquids and gases are trapped against the salt.

Halite is most famous for preserving food and adding flavour as table salt. It is estimated that the average person uses 5.5 kilograms of salt each year. Salt has many uses. For example, in winter, salt is mixed with sand and spread on roads to help keep cars on the road. Because there is no substitute for salt, it has always been valuable to humans.

Photo: Royal Ontario Museum

Halides

Dolomite

Carbonate – Dolomite – CaMg(CO$_3$)$_2$
Family and Crystal System: Carbonate; trigonal (three out of four **axes** lie on the same plane, are of equal lengths, and intersect at 120°; fourth axis not the same length and not perpendicular)

Appearance

Dolomite will often form good **crystals**, which look like squashed cubes. Occasionally the crystal faces are curved and create a saddlelike appearance. **Twinning** is common. Dolomite also occurs in **massive** and fine to coarsely **granular**, but compacted, forms. Usually dolomite is white or grey, but it may be greenish, brownish, or pinkish. It has a glassy **lustre** and is **translucent** to transparent.

Physical Properties

Dolomite is not hard, measuring 3.5 to 4 on the **Mohs scale**. The **specific gravity** is 2.9, which is average. Dolomite is not particularly light or heavy compared to most other minerals. If cold hydrochloric acid is dropped onto dolomite it will not fizz.

Photo: Danny Christopher

Environment & Occurrence

Dolomite may be found in **sedimentary** rocks. It is also a key mineral in dolomitic marble, which is a **metamorphic** rock created from a sedimentary rock. Dolomite forms in **veins** that are created by the movement of hot water and elements through cracks in a rock. In particular, in veins, it occurs with barite and fluorite, as well as other minerals containing lead and zinc.

The rocks that host lead and silver minerals at the former Nanisivik mine, near Arctic Bay, are dolomite-rich limestones. From 1977 to 2002, this mine operated as an underground mine and produced high-quality dolomite, pyrite, galena, and sphalerite crystals.

Did You Know?

Dolomite is quarried to make stone blocks and to manufacture special forms of cement.

Photo: Royal Ontario Museum

Carbonates

Gypsum

Sulphate – Gypsum – $CaSO_4 \cdot 2H_2O$
Alternate Names: Selenite; alabaster; satin spar
Family and Crystal System: Sulphate; monoclinic (three **axes** all of different lengths; two axes perpendicular; third axis inclined)

Appearance

Gypsum **crystals** are common and generally simple. They are usually **tabular** and may be curved or bent. **Twin** crystals are common, with the **swallowtail** variety forming large V-indented outlines, like the tail feathers of a swallow. Gypsum also forms **granular** masses, dense masses, **fibrous** clusters, and **concretionary aggregates**, in which mineral grows in layers outward from a **nucleus**, like a jawbreaker candy, or a surface, like a thin stack of pancakes. Gypsum is usually colourless, white, or grey, but it is also sometimes yellow, red, or brown. Grains are transparent to **translucent**.

Photo: Royal Ontario Museum

Physical Properties

Gypsum breaks easily. It has one **perfect cleavage** and two other **distinct cleavages**. The thin sheets that cleave off are flexible but inelastic. Gypsum can have a glassy, pearly, or silky **lustre**. It is a soft mineral, rated 2 out of 10 on the **Mohs scale**. With a **specific gravity** of 2.3, gypsum is also a lightweight mineral.

Sometimes gypsum is **fluorescent**, and under an ultraviolet light an unusual hourglass shape in the centre of the crystal may be seen.

Environment & Occurrence

Gypsum is a mineral that is deposited from the evaporation of sea water in shallow marine environments. It forms large, extensive beds of relatively pure material. These beds are intermixed with other **sedimentary** layers like salt, clay, and limestone. Gypsum also forms around salt lakes and hot springs. High-quality gypsum crystals can be found in coal beds as well.

Gypsum also forms directly from the mineral anhydrite; if water comes into contact with anhydrite, it converts to gypsum. Selenite is the transparent variety of gypsum, while alabaster is the name for the fine-grained and **massive** form. Satin spar refers to gypsum when it is fibrous. Desert rose or sand rose is the name for gypsum that forms in a desert environment. It generally has a rosette shape (like a rose) and may be coated in sand particles.

On Axel Heiberg Island, west of Ellesmere Island, researchers have been mapping and learning about the gypsum-rich salt **domes** that dot the island. Salty spring water flows out of cracks in the ground. Alabaster is associated with halite **deposits**, and carvers from Resolute have already been asked to test this material for its carving potential.

Did You Know?

The name gypsum comes from the Greek word, *gypsos*, which means plaster. When gypsum is heated, it evaporates 75% of its water and the product is a dry powder called plaster of Paris. When water is added to the powder, it reverts to gypsum and, in the process, recrystallizes into a tightly interlocking substance. Plaster of Paris is used to

Sulphates

make casts to protect broken arms or legs. It also goes into the manufacture of cement, tiles, and wallboard, and is a filler for paints and paper. Gypsum is also used to fertilize **soil**.

Alabaster is used as a carving and ornamental stone by sculptors. Sometimes the alabaster has a banded appearance, which adds an interesting texture and colour to a carving.

Photo: Danny Christopher

Photo: Royal Ontario Museum

Sulphates

Apatite

Phosphate – Apatite – $Ca_5(PO_4)_3(F,OH,Cl)$
Alternate Names: Asparagus stone (green); moroxite (blue green)
Family and Crystal System: Phosphate; **hexagonal** (three out of four **axes** lie on the same plane, are of equal lengths, and intersect at 120°; fourth axis not of the same length and not perpendicular)

Appearance

High-quality **crystals** are quite common. Short to long prisms (six-sided, tubelike crystals) are frequently found. **Tabular** apatite is also common. Sometimes the apatite occurs in **granular** masses, in which the individual crystals are hard to distinguish.

A wide range of colours are represented, including brown, red, violet, yellow green, grey green, and blue green. Apatite may also be colourless, or the grains may often appear dirty. Their **lustre** is a greasy, **vitreous** one. Crystals are **translucent** to transparent.

Physical Properties

Apatite has a **hardness** of 5 and a **specific gravity** of 3.2. There is no **distinct cleavage** and any fracture is uneven, or **conchoidal**. Occasionally apatite is **fluorescent** orange yellow.

Photo: Royal Ontario Museum

Environment & Occurrence

This common mineral occurs in many different rock types, but generally only as an accessory mineral (not a key constituent, but present in tiny quantities). In pegmatites and in **veins**, apatite is very common and can grow to a large size. **Igneous intrusive rocks** with a lot of sodium and potassium are key locations for the formation of apatite.

In sea water, when the teeth and bones of animals fall to the sea floor and mix with guano (bird droppings), a very fine-grained apatite **crystallizes**. As this material builds up, it forms layers.

Did You Know?

The Greek word *apatan*, to deceive, was used to name this mineral because it is often confused with other minerals. Almost all the apatite mined worldwide goes into the production of fertilizer. The agriculture industry uses this fertilizer to increase crop yields and produce more food. Without apatite the planet could not support its population, but fortunately it occurs worldwide.

Photo: Danny Christopher

Phosphates

Actinolite

Silicate – Actinolite – $Ca_2(Mg,Fe^{2+})_5Si_8O_{22}(OH)_2$
Alternate Names: Byssolite
Family and Crystal System: Silicate; amphibole group; monoclinic (three **axes** of **symmetry** all of different lengths; two axes perpendicular; third axis is inclined)

Appearance

This mineral is chemically and physically related to tremolite and is therefore very similar in appearance. The main difference between actinolite and tremolite is that actinolite is usually light to dark green or nearly black, while tremolite is white. If scratched against unglazed porcelain, actinolite will leave a colourless **streak**.

Physical Properties

If fractured, actinolite is splintery or uneven. Actinolite measures 5.5 to 6 on the **Mohs scale**. Actinolite is in the 3 to 3.4 range of **specific gravity**.

Environment & Occurrence

Actinolite is commonly observed in rocks within the region immediately around an **igneous intrusion**. An intrusion is a large body of **magma** that has cooled down and solidified within the **crust**. The heat that this magma emits bakes the surrounding rocks, causing changes in the minerals within these rocks. Actinolite is usually found with muscovite and plagioclase. In **regional metamorphic** rocks, actinolite can be found along with plagioclase, chlorite, and epidote.

Photo: Royal Ontario Museum

Deep green actinolite occurs in serpentinite.

Just west of Rankin Inlet, at the West Meliadine project, one of the most common rock types is amphibolite schist. It contains a large percentage of actinolite, in areas where the **metamorphism** occurred and crustal temperatures and pressures were somewhat above normal. When the temperatures and pressures increase, actinolite is replaced in the schist by hornblende, which is another type of amphibole mineral. A schist is a rock in which the **platy** minerals are lined up parallel to one another, like pages in a book.

Did You Know?

Nephrite is the name given to a mixture of tremolite and actinolite. Nephrite is one type of jade, which is a highly prized stone for carving, jewellery, and other ornamental work. In Asia, nephrite has been used for several thousand years for carving.

Photo: Danny Christopher

Silicates

Andalusite

Silicate – Andalusite – Al_2SiO_5
Alternate Names: Chiastolite
Family and Crystal System: Silicate; **orthorhombic** (three **axes** all of different lengths and all perpendicular to one another)

Appearance

Simple elongated prisms (six-sided, tubelike **crystals**) are common. Andalusite has a square cross-section. The outer surface of andalusite is often covered in muscovite. Andalusite is normally grey, pink, dirty green, brown, or red. The **lustre** is **vitreous**. Grains are nearly **opaque** to **translucent** or, rarely, transparent.

Physical Properties

Andalusite is a hard mineral, measuring 7.5 on the **Mohs scale**. Andalusite has a 3.2 **specific gravity**. A lengthwise **cleavage** is well developed. Chiastolite is the name given to andalusite with **inclusions** of carbon-rich materials that tend to form a cross on the base.

Environment & Occurrence

Andalusite is a characteristic mineral in aluminum-rich **contact metamorphic** rocks, such as shale and hornfels. Andalusite also forms in **regional metamorphic** rocks, such as pelites and gneiss, which have formed under low pressures. Andalusite occurs in granitic pegmatites with quartz, microcline, and muscovite. It can also be found in some **hydrothermal veins**, which are formed by the circulation of hot hydrothermal fluids that trickle off from where **magma** collects in the Earth's **crust**, starts to cool, and forms rocks.

Andalusite is closely related to two other minerals, kyanite and sillimanite, which have the same chemical formula, but different arrangements of **ions** (electrically charged **atoms**). The differences between these three minerals are due to the differences in temperature and pressure in the environment at the time each mineral was formed. The relationship between environmental conditions and specific mineral identification is vital to understanding geological principles.

In the Chantrey Inlet area, north of Garnet Point, a large quantity of chiastolite occurs in a 10-metre-wide layer of pelite.

Photo: Danny Christopher

Did You Know?

Andalusite is used to produce the porcelain needed in the manufacture of spark plugs. Green transparent andalusite may be used as a **gemstone** and is prized for its green to pink **iridescence**.

Silicates

Biotite

Silicate – Biotite – $K(Mg,Fe^{2+})_3(Al,Fe^{3+})Si_3O_{10}(OH,F)_2$
Alternate Name: Biotite mica
Family and Crystal System: Silicate; monoclinic (three **axes** of **symmetry** all of different lengths; two axes perpendicular; third axis is inclined)

Appearance

Biotite can be irregular or **platy**, or can occur in widely scattered flakes. Normally black, dark brown, or greenish black, the **crystals** are also transparent to **translucent**. The **lustre** of biotite is **vitreous** to **sub-metallic** (somewhat resembling a metal). Well-formed crystals are rare but, when they occur, they are barrel-shaped.

Physical Properties

Biotite splits very easily into flakes, thus having **perfect cleavage**. Biotite has only one direction along which these breaks will happen. The cleavage sheets are both flexible and elastic; however, not many minerals are. On the **Mohs scale**, this mineral has a **hardness** of 2.5 to 3 and a 2.7 to 3.3 range of **specific gravity**. If fractured, it breaks in an uneven pattern.

Photo: Royal Ontario Museum

Environment & Occurrence

Biotite can be found in all three of the major rock types: **igneous**, **sedimentary**, and **metamorphic**. Of the rocks that formed inside the Earth's **crust** (**intrusive**), biotite is common in granite, syenite, diorite, and gabbro. Biotite creates the dark, speckled look of the rock. Biotite also occurs in the **volcanic**, finer-grained equivalents, such as rhyolite, andesite, and basalt. In sedimentary rocks, such as sandstone, biotite is found in small quantities. It is very common in metamorphic rocks, such as schist, hornfels, and gneiss.

At the Ulu gold **deposit**, just south of Coronation Gulf, biotite occurs in a variety of ways. In proximity to the gold **ore deposits**, there is a basalt deposit that has been deformed by squeezing and altered by the percolation of hot liquids, the result of which has been the introduction of new minerals. Bands rich in biotite formed on either side of the main gold zone. In the surrounding area there are many sedimentary rocks, among them a turbiditic greywacke with abundant quartz, and biotite. Gabbro **sills** (a **tabular** sheet of **igneous** rock that is intruded between and parallel to the existing rock layers) at Ulu contain biotite **megacrysts**, which are very large crystals.

Did You Know?

Insulation for electrical equipment is made from biotite. It is also added to gypsum wallboard and other construction materials (masonry and concrete blocks) as a filler. In paint, biotite acts as a thickener and makes it weatherproof. As well, in the manufacture of wallpaper, biotite gives the surface a silky or shiny lustre.

Photo: Danny Christopher

Silicates

Chlorite

Silicate – Chlorite – $(Mg,Fe,Al,Li,Mn,Ni)_{4-6}(Si,Al,B,Fe)_4O_{10}(OH,O)_8$
Alternate Names: Clinochore; chamosite
Family and Crystal System: Silicate; triclinic or monoclinic (all three **axes** are of different lengths and are all inclined to one another; or three axes all of different lengths; two axes perpendicular; third axis is inclined)

Appearance

Good quality **crystals** of chlorite are rare, and chlorite generally forms **platy** or scaly **aggregates**. It can also be scattered as single flakes throughout the rock. It is rare to find a **hexagonal** or pseudo-hexagonal (not quite perfectly six-sided) crystal, but they do exist. Chlorite is normally green, but sometimes it is yellow, brown, pink, red, white, or violet. The **lustre** is **vitreous** or dull, and flakes are **translucent** or **opaque**.

Physical Properties

Although the minerals in this group have diverse formulas, they all have very similar properties, which makes it hard to tell them apart. For this reason, it is generally adequate to refer to all the minerals in this group simply as chlorite.

The mineral breaks easily into sheets in one direction, displaying a **perfect cleavage**. The cleavage flakes bend, but they do not spring back to their original shape, so they are inelastic. If scratched over a piece of porcelain, the mineral's resulting **streak** is grey green or brown.

Chlorite is quite soft, and has a **hardness** of 2.5 on the **Mohs scale**. The measured **specific gravity** is 2.7 to 2.9, so the mineral has a moderate weight.

Photo: Danny Christopher

Environment & Occurrence

Chlorite minerals occur in a wide variety of rock types. Commonly, amphibole, pyroxene, and biotite become chlorite. This alteration may happen when the pressure affecting the rock changes. Chlorite can also be found in **metamorphic** and **sedimentary** rocks. In low-grade metamorphic rocks (those that have not been changed to any great extent), chlorite occurs in a chlorite schist. A schist is a rock in which the platy minerals are all lined up and are parallel to one another.

Just northwest of Rankin Inlet on the Meliadine project, chlorite is found in a variety of environments. It occurs in a sedimentary rock called greywacke and in **volcanic** rocks that have undergone slight **metamorphism** (changes or alterations). The pillowed basalt, **massive** basalt, gabbro, and volcaniclastic rocks all contain significant amounts of chlorite. As well, the iron formation rocks contain some chlorite.

Did You Know?

Chlorite contributes to the green colour of many rocks. Chlorite is used to make a reflective green pigment in the manufacture of wallpaper. Some chlorite masses are easy to carve.

Photo: Royal Ontario Museum

Silicates

Epidote

Silicate – Epidote – $Ca_2(Fe^{3+},Al)_3(Si_2O_7)(SiO_4)(O,OH)_2$
Alternate Names: Clinozoisite
Family and Crystal System: Silicate; monoclinic (three **axes** all of different lengths; two axes perpendicular; third axis inclined)

Appearance

Epidote generally forms **crystals** that are **prismatic, tabular,** or **acicular**. It can also form in **granular** masses or even **fibrous** aggregates. Sometimes the lengthwise direction is also marked by **striations**. Epidote is pistachio green, brownish green, dark green, or almost black. The surface appears glassy and usually the grains are **translucent**.

Photo: Royal Ontario Museum

Physical Properties

There are two **cleavage** directions present in epidote: one that is good (in which the mineral breaks easily and clearly) and one that is poor (in which the mineral breaks in a less obvious way, yet still with a well-defined geometry). The **hardness** of this mineral is 6 to 7 on the **Mohs scale** of hardness and its **specific gravity** is 3.4.

Environment & Occurrence

Epidote is a common mineral and is most often found in **regional metamorphic** rocks. It occurs in albite, quartz, calcium-rich amphiboles, and chlorite. Epidote commonly fills narrow, small **veins** running through granite, syenite, and granodiorite. In basalt, epidote is found in **gas** bubble cavities with calcite and zeolite minerals. In **contact metamorphic** limestones, epidote is found with iron-bearing minerals.

Clinozoisite is a related mineral that has little or no iron. It is a lighter green but otherwise looks very similar to epidote.

On the northeast end of Walrus Island, along the east coast of James Bay, there is an augite syenite that contains abundant epidote. A diabase **dike** cross-cuts the syenite, and the epidote forms a halo around this diabase. The grains occur as interlacing radiating crystals and are light to dark yellowish green.

Did You Know?

Due to its relative hardness, epidote may be used as a gem if the transparency is high and the colour is good.

Epidote is one of the minerals that contributes to the green colour in the range of rocks in a greenstone belt. The other minerals that also contribute to the green colour are chlorite, hornblende, and actinolite. Greenstone belts are those areas of ancient rock that consist mostly of **volcanic** and **sedimentary** rocks that have been affected by **regional metamorphism**.

Photo: Danny Christopher

Silicates

Garnet

Silicate – Garnet – $(Ca, Fe^{2+}, Mg, Mn)_3(Al, Cr, Fe^{3+}, Mn^{3+}, Ti, V^{3+})_2(SiO_4)_3$
Alternate Names: Pyrope; almandine; spessartine; andradite; uvarovite; grossular
Family and Crystal System: Silicate; garnet group; cubic (three **axes** of equal lengths all perpendicular to one another)

Appearance

Garnet is the name for a group of related minerals. These minerals are **equant**. **Crystals** with some flat faces (like those on soccer balls) are readily found. Most grains are red to brown, but a huge range of colour can be found, depending on slight changes in the chemical formula of the mineral. For example, pyrope is a deep red to almost black garnet; almandine is red to brown; spessartine is orange, red, or brown; grossular is white, yellow, pink, green, or brown; andradite is yellow, green, brown, or black; and finally, uvarovite is a lovely emerald green colour. The **lustre** of the mineral is generally **vitreous**. Garnet is **translucent** to transparent.

Physical Properties

Garnet ranks 7 on the **Mohs scale**. The **specific gravity** of this mineral ranges from 3.5 to 4.3, which makes it heavier than the average common mineral. If a garnet grain is fractured, the fracture will have a **conchoidal** shape.

Environment & Occurrence

Garnet is a widespread mineral and is most often found in **metamorphic** rocks. The common variety, almandine, occurs in **sediments**, metamorphic gneiss, and schist. Pyrope, the other abundant garnet, is found in **igneous** rocks such as peridotite, serpentinite, and kimberlite.

Photo: Royal Ontario Museum

Just west of Rankin Inlet at the West Meliadine gold project, **sedimentary** rocks that have been metamorphosed (affected by changes in temperature and/or pressure) contain some garnets. At the West Meliadine gold project, there is also a greywacke that has been converted to schist and gneiss, which has large garnet grains.

The iron formation, when highly metamorphosed, also contains significant amounts of garnet.

Did You Know?

Photo: Royal Ontario Museum

The name garnet is derived from the Latin word *granatum*, which stands for pomegranate. The seeds of this fruit resemble garnet in colour and shape. Because of garnet's **hardness** and its lovely variety of colours (it occurs in every colour except blue), it is in high demand for use in jewellery.

Garnet is also mined for use in a type of sandpaper (called garnet paper) and other abrasives.

Photo: Danny Christopher

Silicates

Hornblende

Silicate – Hornblende – $Ca_2(Fe^{2+},Mg)_4(Al,Fe^{3+})(Si_7Al)O_{22}(OH)_2$
Alternate Names: Ferrohornblende; magnesiohornblende; common hornblende
Family and Crystal System: Silicate; amphibole group; monoclinic (three **axes** of **symmetry** all of different lengths; two axes perpendicular; third axis inclined)

Appearance

Hornblende is generally dark green to black. **Crystals** are relatively common and form prisms (six-sided, tubelike crystals) or **columnar** aggregates (columnlike groupings). Sometimes long, thin crystals radiate out in a fan shape. An end section, for example, is six-sided. The **lustre** of the crystals is **vitreous**, or, rarely, milky. Grains will range from **opaque** to **translucent**. Hornblende varies widely in terms of how much light will pass through its grains.

Photo: Danny Christopher

Physical Properties

Hornblende has a **hardness** of 5.5 to 6 on the **Mohs scale** of hardness and 3 to 3.4 is the range of its **specific gravity**. It displays two **perfect cleavages** of 56° that intersect. The fracture pattern of hornblende is uneven, with no particular pattern. If the edge of a grain is scratched against a piece of porcelain, the resulting **streak** of powder is grey green or grey brown.

Environment & Occurrence

Hornblende minerals are common and occur frequently in **metamorphic** rocks, such as hornblende schist and amphibolite. Sometimes rocks are composed entirely of hornblende minerals. They are also found in **igneous** rocks, namely basalts, granites, syenites, and pegmatites.

Ferguson Lake is situated about 70 kilometres west of Rankin Inlet. East of the lake there is a large body of rock called the Uligataalik Hill Syenite. This is an **intrusive** igneous rock, which means it was formed from molten **magma** under the surface of the Earth. This syenite contains orthoclase, quartz, and plenty of hornblende.

Did You Know?

The composition of hornblende can be quite variable. At the time of crystallization, hornblende will incorporate many of the chemicals that are available, even if only in tiny amounts. Because of this characteristic, hornblende is a very useful mineral for geologists called petrologists who examine rocks in detail. Petrologists find the nature of the hornblende informative in terms of describing the magma conditions at the time of formation.

Silicates

Kyanite

Silicate – Kyanite – Al$_2$SiO$_5$
Alternate Names: Disthene; cyanite
Family and Crystal System: Silicate; triclinic (all three **axes** are of different lengths and are all inclined to one another)

Appearance

Kyanite normally forms **prismatic crystals**. It may also form clumps of bladelike grains. Crystals are often twisted or bent. Most commonly a blue colour is observed, but kyanite may be white, grey, or greenish (and rarely yellow, pink, or almost black). Different colours may be present in a single crystal. The light bouncing off the **cleavage** faces gives a glassy or pearly **lustre**. Crystals are **translucent** to transparent. Occasionally there are fine **striations** (scratches or fine parallel lines) across the short dimension of the prism.

Physical Properties

Kyanite's cleavage is perfect, and forms large rectangular faces. A unique property of kyanite is its variable **hardness**, which depends on the direction in which it is scratched. Across the crystal the hardness is 6.5, which is quite hard. If scratched lengthwise, however, its hardness is 4.5. The **specific gravity** of kyanite is 3.6 and, if a grain fractures, it reveals a **fibrous** break.

Photo: Royal Ontario Museum

Environment & Occurrence

Kyanite forms in aluminum-rich **metamorphic** rocks, such as mica schists, gneiss, and eclogite. Kyanite is closely related to two other minerals, andalusite and sillimanite, which have the same chemical formula as kyanite, but a different arrangement of **ions** (electrically charged **atoms**). These differences are due to the temperature and pressure in the environment at the time the mineral was formed. The relationship between environmental conditions and specific mineral identification is vital to understanding geological principles.

One very unusual **occurrence** of kyanite in Nunavut is in the Jericho kimberlite **pipe**, at Contwoyto Lake, in the Kitikmeot region. Kyanite occurs there in chunks of eclogite rock, which were caught up in the kimberlite as it rose explosively through the Earth's upper **mantle** and **crust**. Besides the kyanite eclogite, geologists working at this project found diamond eclogite, apatite eclogite, and zircon eclogite, which are all unusual eclogite variations.

Photo: Danny Christopher

Did You Know?

Kyanite is used in the production of porcelain. Porcelain is a strong, heat-resistant material and can withstand the action of chemicals. Kyanite is used to make high temperature bricks and spark plugs. It also makes a perfect electrical insulator. Clear, large stones of intense colour are used as **gemstones**.

Silicates

Muscovite

Silicate – Muscovite – $KAl_2(Si_3Al)O_{10}(OH,F)_2$
Alternate Names: White mica; muscovy glass
Family and Crystal System: Silicate; monoclinic (three **axes** of **symmetry** all of different lengths; two axes perpendicular; third axis inclined)

Appearance

Crystals occur in **tabular** shapes with **hexagonal** outlines. Muscovite also occurs as tiny scattered flakes or as **scaly** aggregates. On rare occasions, a high-quality crystal may appear as a cone-shaped prism. Generally muscovite is colourless, but it can be very pale yellow, green, or brown. The **lustre** is **vitreous** to pearly and the grains are transparent to **translucent**.

Physical Properties

There is one **perfect cleavage** in muscovite, which helps to create the thin elastic flakes. Muscovite registers 2 to 2.5 on the **Mohs scale** and has a **specific gravity** of 2.8.

Photo: Danny Christopher

Environment & Occurrence

This common mineral is found in granites and pegmatites, both **igneous** rocks. It may also be found in many **metamorphic** rocks, such as mica schists and gneiss. When muscovite is very fine-grained, it is called sericite. Sericite is common as an **alteration product**, created from the breakdown of feldspars (plagioclase or orthoclase) and other aluminum-rich minerals. Muscovite itself resists **erosion** and can often be found in sands. In **sedimentary** rocks, muscovite is a common constituent of shale.

Muscovite is the most common mica and can be found in many places. There is an **occurrence** at the Meadowbank gold project, close to Baker Lake, for example. Between the North Portage and Vault gold **deposits** there is also a high ridge of white quartzite rock where muscovite and epidote-rich layers, mixed with the quartz-rich layers, appear in bands.

Did You Know?

This mineral is named after a former Russian province called Muscovy. The people there used muscovite in their windows and called it muscovy glass. These days, muscovite is used by the electrical industry because it acts as an insulator and is not flammable. Because of these properties, muscovite was also used in the windows of cooking and wood stoves. Muscovite also makes its way into the manufacture of paper, rubber, fireproof paint, and the fake snow that gets sprayed onto Christmas trees.

Photo: Royal Ontario Museum

Silicates

Nepheline

Silicate – Nepheline – $(Na,K)AlSiO_4$
Family and Crystal System: Silicate; **hexagonal** (three out of four **axes** lie on the same plane, are of equal lengths, and intersect at 120°; fourth axis not of the same length and not perpendicular)

Appearance

Nepheline **crystals** are rare and this mineral can mostly be found in irregular masses and in very small, scattered grains. If a small crystal is found, it will be short and **columnar** and may have short, angled faces at the ends. Nepheline is typically colourless, white, or grey. Occasionally it will be somewhat brownish, greenish, or reddish. It has a greasy look or **lustre** to it. Grains are **translucent** to transparent.

Photo: Royal Ontario Museum

Physical Properties

Nepheline is relatively hard, measuring 6 on the **Mohs scale**. With a **standard gravity** of 2.6, nepheline is also of average density. The fracture pattern is **conchoidal**. Portions of nepheline crystals may be **fluorescent** in the orange red colours. Nepheline has one **indistinct cleavage**.

Photo: Royal Ontario Museum

Environment & Occurrence

Nepheline is found in **igneous** rocks that are low in silica content. These silica-poor rocks are called nepheline syenite and, in them, the nepheline replaces some of the feldspar (either plagioclase or orthoclase) minerals that would normally occur. This mineral can also occur in nepheline syenite pegmatites, which are very coarse-grained equivalents of the syenite.

Nepheline and the nepheline syenite rock are rare. White nepheline is known from two **occurrences** of lapis lazuli 15 kilometres north of Kimmirut. Small bodies of syenite do occur in this area, and some nepheline is also found in the marble near the sapphire occurrences at Kimmirut.

Did You Know?

The name nepheline is derived from the Greek word *nephele*, which means cloud. Nepheline was given this name for the cloudy appearance it develops when the mineral is placed in a strong acid.

Nepheline and quartz do not ever occur in the same rock together—this is useful diagnostic information, although it can be hard to tell the two rocks apart. Nepheline is softer and can be scratched with a penknife.

Nepheline is mined for use in the glass and ceramic industries.

Silicates

Olivine

Silicate – Olivine – (Mg,Fe,Mn,Ni)2SiO4
Alternate Names: Fayalite; forsterite, peridot
Family and Crystal System: Silicate; **orthorhombic** (three **axes** all of different lengths, perpendicular to one another)

Appearance

Olivine generally occurs as a mass of grains. When larger grains are present, **prismatic** shapes ranging from stubby and boxlike to long bars with two pyramid shapes at opposite ends can be observed. The grains reflect light just like glass, which is called having a **vitreous lustre**. Olivine is **translucent** to transparent. The predominant colours are olive green (hence the name), yellowish green, and brown to black. Gem-quality olivine, called peridot, is flawless and clear.

Photo: Royal Ontario Museum

Physical Properties

Olivine is quite hard, measuring 6.5 to 7 on the **Mohs scale**. It cannot be scratched with a knife. The fracture pattern is **conchoidal**. The **specific gravity** is fairly high, at 3.3 to 4.4, which means the **crystals** will feel heavy. This range is based on how much iron is contained within the microscopic structure of the crystal. The higher the iron content, the heavier the crystal. The heavier mineral is called fayalite.

Environment & Occurrence

Olivine is quite abundant in very dark-coloured **igneous** rocks like peridotite and basalt. A rock type called dunite is made up almost entirely of olivine. In metamorphosed dolomites, the magnesium-rich olivine forsterite, is common.

Just south of Kugluktuk is the very large **igneous intrusion** known as the Muskox intrusion. An intrusion is a large body of rock that has formed from the cooling and solidification of **magma** underground. In the central core of this body, there are dunites made up almost entirely of olivine, peridotite, and chromite (a mineral containing chromium) layers. Associated with these rocks are significant **deposits** of palladium, platinum, nickel, and copper; all of these are valuable and important metals.

Did You Know?

Peridot, the gem quality olivine, comes in shades of yellow green, olive green, or greenish brown. The gem is quite hard, which means the crystal cannot be easily scratched. **Gemstones** like peridot—the August birthstone—are usually difficult to scratch, which is part of their sturdy allure.

When peridot is viewed in the moonlight it loses its yellow tint and has been called evening emerald. However, it is misleading to call peridot an emerald since the emerald is actually a mineral called beryl.

Photo: Danny Christopher

Silicates

Orthoclase

Silicate – Orthoclase – $KAlSi_3O_8$
Alternate Names: Perthite; alkali feldspar; potassium feldspar
Family and Crystal System: Silicate; feldspar group; monoclinic (three **axes** all of different lengths; two axes perpendicular; third axis inclined)

Appearance

Orthoclase forms long and narrow **crystals** with flat, nearly square cross-sections. **Twins** are common. Orthoclase can also be found scattered throughout rocks, or as coarse-grained masses.

Orthoclase is a slight fleshy pink to red colour, but it can also be colourless, white, grey, yellow, blue, or green. This mineral's **lustre** is **vitreous**, although on the **cleavage plane**, where it naturally fractures, it will look pearly. Most grains are **translucent**.

Physical Properties

Orthoclase is 6 to 6.5 on the **Mohs scale**, too hard to scratch with a penknife. The **specific gravity** is 2.6, as it is a fairly light mineral. The fracture pattern is **conchoidal** to uneven (having no pattern). Three cleavages range from perfect to indistinct. Cleavages are the way a mineral breaks along well-defined planes of weakness. A **perfect cleavage** means the mineral is very likely to break along these planes. By contrast, when the cleavage is **indistinct**, the mineral will occasionally break along these preferred planes.

Photo: Royal Ontario Museum

Environment & Occurrence

Orthoclase is a very common mineral in granite, pegmatite, and syenite, and its pigment contributes to its fleshy pink or brick red colour. Orthoclase can also be found in a few **sedimentary** rocks and in many **metamorphic** rocks, such as gneiss and schist.

In and around Iqaluit, hill after hill of granodiorite gneiss can be found. This metamorphic rock has a great deal of orthoclase in it. Look for the pink grains that are clustered into **streaks**. The weathered face of this rock may not initially impress, but the cut and polished stone is very attractive, which is why it is sometimes used for making countertop tiles and boardroom tables.

Did You Know?

A single grain can contain two minerals, orthoclase and plagioclase, which act like oil and vinegar and separate into tiger stripes. Sometimes this separation is visible with the naked eye, and when this separation occurs, the mineral is then called perthite.

The lovelier orthoclase stones are used for jewellery due to their **hardness**. Otherwise, most orthoclase is used to manufacture ceramic and glass.

Photo: Danny Christopher

Silicates

Phlogopite

Silicate – Phlogopite – $K(Mg,Fe^{2+})_3Si_3AlO_{10}(F,OH)_2$
Alternate Names: Mica
Family and Crystal System: Silicate; monoclinic (three **axes** all of different lengths; two axes perpendicular; third axis inclined)

Appearance

Phlogopite **crystals** are usually **tabular**. Their outline may approach a **hexagonal** shape. The **prismatic** form is fairly common. Masses of phlogopite will stack together, forming bands or **platy** clumps. The colour is pale yellow to pale brown, sometimes with a greenish or reddish cast. The **lustre** is glassy to pearly, or even **sub-metallic**. Thin sheets of phlogopite will be transparent. Sometimes a starlike figure, called an **asterism**, can be seen in this mineral.

Physical Properties

The **cleavage** is perfect in one direction with phlogopite. The very thin sheets are both flexible and elastic. On the **Mohs scale**, phlogopite has a range of 2.5 to 3 and a **specific gravity** of 2.9.

Environment & Occurrence

Phlogopite occurs in rocks that are rich in magnesium, such as peridotites, pegmatites, and kimberlites. Phlogopite also occurs in metamorphosed dolostone. Near Kimmirut, the marbles that host the sapphire mineral **occurrences** also contain abundant phlogopite. There are some localities along the Soper River where dinner plate–sized crystals can be found.

Photo: Danny Christopher

108

Photo: Royal Ontario Museum

Did You Know?

The name phlogopite is derived from the Greek word *phlogos*, or firelike, due to the reddish glow it often displays.

A peculiar physical property is its triboluminescence, which means that sparks of light may be produced by striking the mineral with a metal point. The edges of the sheets may even glow when they are pulled apart. Because the physical properties of phlogopite are very similar to muscovite, the uses of this mineral in industry are much the same. For example, phlogopite, like muscovite, is used by the electrical industry because it acts as an insulator and is not flammable.

The largest phlogopite crystal ever found came from the Lacy mine in Ontario, Canada, weighing in at a stunning 75 tonnes and measuring 11 by 4.5 metres. Now that's a crystal!

Silicates

Plagioclase

Silicate – Plagioclase – $(Na,Ca)Al(Al,Si)Si_2O_8$
Alternate Names: Albite (Na-rich); anorthite (Ca-rich)
Family and Crystal System: Silicate; feldspar group; triclinic (all three **axes** are of different lengths and are all inclined towards one another)

Appearance

Plagioclase usually occurs as small grains scattered throughout the rock, or it may form coarse-grained masses. Individual **crystals**, though rare, are **tabular**. **Twinning** of crystals is very common and the resulting appearance is like the slightly fanned pages in a book. The common colour for plagioclase is colourless, white, or grey. Very rarely it is greenish, bluish, or reddish. Crystals have a **vitreous lustre** and are mostly **translucent**.

Physical Properties

Plagioclase is relatively hard, ranking 6 on the **Mohs scale**. The **specific gravity** of plagioclase is 2.6 and the fracture pattern is uneven, having no particular pattern. Two **good cleavages** are evident in plagioclase. Along the **cleavage planes**, the lustre is pearly. The cleavages are oriented at nearly 90° to one another.

Photo: Royal Ontario Museum

Plagioclase is the name of a series of feldspar minerals. The six members are albite, oligoclase, andesine, labradorite, bytownite, and anorthite. Although they vary slightly in chemistry, their physical properties are very similar, making them hard to distinguish without chemical or optical tests.

The plagioclases are the most important rock-forming minerals. They are so prevalent in **igneous** rocks that most classification schemes are based on the quantity and type of plagioclase contained in any igneous rock. In general, the more silica-rich the rock, the more likely it is to contain the sodium-rich plagioclase (albite). Conversely, the less silica-rich the rock, the greater the chance it will contain anorthite, the calcium-rich member.

Albite is commonly found in pegmatites, in which the crystals are large. Albite is also common in **metamorphic** schist and gneiss. Anorthite can often be found in limestone that has been affected by **contact metamorphism**.

Plagioclase is also found in **sedimentary** rocks, especially in greywacke and sandstone.

Almost any rock in Nunavut may contain plagioclase. If a mineral in the rock is light-coloured, and cannot be scratched with a penknife, then it may well be plagioclase. Look for the very fine **striations**, which are the edges of twinned crystals. Keep in mind that these striations will not always be developed.

Did You Know?

One variety of plagioclase is called labradorite and displays a lovely blue play of colour. It is found in eastern Labrador, near Nain. This stone is commonly used for jewellery and for some ornamental work. Moonstone is the name given to a plagioclase when it displays a bluish, milky tint. Sunstone is a plagioclase that has tiny specks of hematite or mica, causing it to sparkle. Both moonstone and sunstone can be used to make jewellery.

The coarse-grained plagioclase, from pegmatite bodies, is used in the manufacture of porcelain, enamel, and glass.

Silicates

Pyroxene

Silicate – Pyroxene – $(Ca,Mg,Fe^{2+},Mn,Na,Li)(Al,Mg,Fe^{3+},Mn,Cr,Sc,Ti)(Si,Al)_2O_6$
Alternate Names: Diopside; hedenbergite; augite; chrome diopside; enstatite
Family and Crystal System: Silicate; pyroxene group; monoclinic (three **axes** all
of different lengths; two axes perpendicular; third axis inclined) and **orthorhombic**
(three axes of equal lengths, and all perpendicular to one another)

Appearance

Crystals are generally **prismatic**. Most
often pyroxene forms **granular** masses or
columnar aggregates.

There are several minerals in the pyroxene
group: diopside is white to light green;
hedenbergite is dark green to black;
chrome diopside is a striking emerald
green; augite is dark green to black; and
enstatite is grey, green, black, or brown. As
with many silicate minerals, the **lustre** is
glassy. Pyroxene can range from **opaque**
to transparent.

Photo: Danny Christopher

Physical Properties

Pyroxenes have two **distinct cleavage planes** that cross at an angle of 93° or 87°,
making the planes appear to be close to right angles. Sometimes there is a **parting** that
cuts across the width of the grain. Parting is a less regular form of cleavage and looks
like fine parallel scratches.

Pyroxene is relatively hard, at 6 on the **Mohs scale**. The **specific gravity** of pyroxene
averages 3.3 and, if a grain fractures, it has an uneven surface, with no regular pattern.
If the grain is dragged across a piece of unglazed porcelain, the powder residue is
coloured. With augite, the resulting **streak** is grey-green. Hedenbergite displays a light
brown streak with green tints. Diopside has a white streak and thus has a similar colour
to the outward appearance of the pyroxene specimen.

Pyroxene minerals occur in calcium-rich **metamorphic** rocks and in limestone that has undergone **contact metamorphism**. Limestone that is changed from the heat becomes marble. **Igneous** rocks rich in magnesium and iron are also ideal places to find pyroxene, as are **intrusive rocks** (formed inside the Earth's **crust**) like gabbro, and **volcanic** rocks like basalt. Omphacite is a rare type of green pyroxene, which occurs alongside garnet in a very strongly metamorphosed rock type called eclogite.

Photo: Royal Ontario Museum

Near Kimmirut is the Beluga sapphire **occurrence**, wherein the rock containing sapphire also contains great amounts of diopside and displays a rare purple colour.

Did You Know?

At times diopside has an intense colour, is very clear, and can be used as a **gemstone**. Jadeite is a pyroxene mineral that develops in serpentinite and can occur in a wide variety of colours. Diopside, and the actinolite variety called nephrite, is termed jade. However, jadeite that is the best quality is referred to as precious jade. Jade is used in jewellery, carving, and other ornamental work. The more transparent the jade, the more valuable it will be.

Silicates

Quartz

Silicate – Quartz – SiO_2
Alternate Names: Rock crystal; milky quartz; amethyst; citrine; smoky quartz; rose quartz; cat's eye; aventurine; chalcedony; carnelian; sard; chrysoprase; plasma; heliotrope; agate; moss agate; onyx; sardonyx; petrified wood; flint; chert; jasper; tiger's eye
Family and Crystal System: Silicate; trigonal (three out of four **axes** lie on the same plane, are of equal lengths, and intersect at 120°; fourth axis is perpendicular and a different length)

Appearance

Quartz **crystals** are common and are **prismatic**, with a six-sided cross-section. Quartz **twins** are also common, although sometimes difficult to see. The sides display crosswise **striations**. Quartz also forms aggregates of regular crystals as well as **microcrystalline** aggregates. This mineral occurs in every possible colour, but mostly it is colourless or white. The **lustre** of quartz is **vitreous**. When in microcrystalline form, the lustre of quartz is slightly greasy.

Physical Properties

Fractures in quartz are **conchoidal**. On the **Mohs scale**, quartz is a 7 and its **specific gravity** is 2.7. Quartz crystals are transparent to **translucent**. This mineral does not display **cleavage**.

Environment & Occurrence

Quartz is found in many geological environments. In **metamorphic** rock, large quantities of quartz occur in gneiss, mica schist, quartzite, and eclogite. In **igneous** rock, quartz is in silica-rich **intrusive rocks** like granodiorite, granite, pegmatites, and **veins**. Because quartz is quite hard, it resists **weathering**, and therefore is found in many **sedimentary** rocks, such as sandstone and conglomerate.

Photo: Danny Christopher

Photo: Royal Ontario Museum

The microcrystalline varieties, like flint and chert, are formed by the accumulation of silica on the sea floor. Agate forms in a cavity in the rock and makes thin **concentric** bands all around the cavity walls. Often in the centre there will be larger quartz crystals.

In the Hope Bay belt, east of Bathurst Inlet, gold occurs in a white quartz **vein**. This vein is over 3 kilometres long and occurs within **folded** and metamorphosed pillow basalts. At the north end, the veins are folded to create a wide, high-grade zone, which lies close to the surface. This gold-rich material will be mined as part of the operation of the Doris North gold mine.

Did You Know?

Most of the coloured varieties of quartz (listed at the top under alternate names) are used frequently as **gemstones** in jewellery. Amethyst (purple quartz) is very popular. Lovely crystals and microcrystalline forms can be carved into amazing sculptures.

In the construction industry, quartz finds many uses in concrete, cement, mortar, and building stone. It is also used to manufacture glass, ceramics, and porcelain.

When electricity is transmitted through a quartz crystal it vibrates at a very specific frequency. This interesting property is used in precise quartz movement watches, radios, televisions, and other electronics. Mostly synthetic quartz, grown in laboratories, is used for resonant frequency.

Silicates

Serpentine

Silicate – Serpentine – $(Mg,Fe,Ni)_3Si_2O_5(OH)_4$
Alternate names: Antigorite; lizardite; chrysotile
Family and Crystal System: Silicate; **orthorhombic** (three **axes** all of different lengths, all perpendicular to one another) and monoclinic (three axes all of different lengths; two axes at right angles; third axis is inclined)

Appearance

Large **crystals** are not found. Instead this mineral forms dense masses or clusters of fibres. Normally this mineral is greenish and mottled, but it can also be yellow, brown, red, or grey. The **lustre** of serpentine is greasy to silky and the grains are **translucent**. If serpentine is found in **vein** form, the fibres will be oriented at right angles to the vein walls.

Physical Properties

On the **Mohs scale**, serpentine varies widely, from 3 to 5. This mineral has a **specific gravity** of 2.6 and a very high flexibility. The **streak** is generally white and shiny.

Environment & Occurrence

Serpentine is a fairly common mineral and can be found in **igneous** and **metamorphic** rocks. It is an **alteration product** of another mineral called olivine, which means that when olivine breaks down, it produces serpentine.

In Nunavut, serpentine is widely used by carvers to produce fabulous figurines. Near Sanikiluaq, at Tukarak Island, a talc and serpentine rock is quarried and then exported to many other places for carvers to use.

Photo: Danny Christopher

The name for this group of minerals is derived from the fact that they look mottled and scaly, like a serpent or snake.

The fibrous variety, chrysotile, was used in building insulation (asbestos) for generations. When it was discovered that the tiny fibres can lodge in the lungs and cause health problems, this insulation was removed.

Photo: Royal Ontario Museum

Silicates

Sillimanite

Silicate – Sillimanite – Al_2SiO_5
Alternate Names: Fibrolite
Family and Crystal System: Silicate; **orthorhombic** (three **axes** all of different lengths, all perpendicular to one another)

Appearance

Sillimanite normally occurs in **fibrous** and **columnar** clumps. High-quality **crystals** are rare, mostly because the ends of the crystals are usually uneven. Sillimanite is grey, white, colourless, blue, yellow, light brown, or green. The way light is reflected off the mineral's surface makes it look like glass. When examining ultrathin fibres, they appear silky. Grains are **translucent** to transparent.

Physical Properties

Sillimanite is quite hard, at 6.5 to 7.5 on the **Mohs scale**. The **specific gravity** is 3.2 and the **streak** is white. It displays one **good cleavage**, which means the mineral breaks easily and clearly.

Environment & Occurrence

Sillimanite is another **metamorphic** mineral related to kyanite and andalusite. It occurs mostly in aluminum-rich rocks that have been affected by high-grade **regional metamorphism**. The typical host rocks are gneiss and mica schist. Sillimanite can also be found in rocks affected by **contact metamorphism** near a large **intrusion**.

Other minerals that occur with sillimanite include corundum, spinel, cordierite, and andalusite.

Photo: Royal Ontario Museum

At Chidliak Bay, at the south end of Baffin Island, there is a sillimanite gneiss. Bladed to **tabular** sillimanite crystals can be found there, grouped in large masses. Crystals measure up to 4 millimetres in length.

Did You Know?

A pale blue, gem-quality sillimanite has been mined from the area of Mogok, Thailand, for use in jewellery.

As with kyanite, when sillimanite occurs in large masses, it is mined to make porcelain and ceramics that are resistant to heat and corrosion by chemicals.

Silicates

Talc

Silicate – Talc – $Mg_3Si_4O_{10}(OH)_2$
Alternate names: Soapstone; steatite
Family and Crystal System: Silicate; monoclinic (three **axes** of **symmetry** all of different lengths; two axes perpendicular; third axis inclined) and triclinic (all three axes are of different lengths and inclined to one another)

Appearance

Talc **crystals** are very rare, and normally talc is found in **platy** or dense, fine-grained masses. Though usually pale green, talc can also be white or grey. The **lustre** is greasy or pearly. Flakes are **translucent**.

Physical Properties

Individual flakes of talc are flexible but inelastic, and they will break if bent too far. There is one **perfect cleavage**. Talc is very **sectile**, meaning it may be cut with a knife without breaking into chunks. On the **Mohs scale**, talc has a **hardness** of 1, which is very low and means that it can be scratched with a fingernail. Talc's **specific gravity** is 2.8, and this mineral also has a distinctly greasy feel.

Photo: Danny Christopher

Environment & Occurrence

Soapstone is the name given to this mineral when it occurs in dense masses. Many Nunavut carvers value soapstone as the best material for their art.

Talc often occurs in **metamorphic** rocks, especially those rich in magnesium. Talc also occurs in smaller quantities from the breaking down of rocks such as peridotite, dunite, and pyroxenite.

Nunavut has many small **occurrences** of talc and soapstone. Unfortunately, some locations are being depleted of this valuable resource. Any new finds

Photo: Royal Ontario Museum

of this carving stone must be reported to the Minerals, Oil and Gas division of the government, to be included in its inventory. The beautiful, bright apple green material from Markham Bay, near Cape Dorset, is in dramatic contrast to the black-and-dark-grey soapstone from around Baker Lake. Anyone who sees many carvings from around Nunavut can soon learn to identify the unique community from which the rock and the art originate.

Did You Know?

In Arabic, the word *talq* means pure—this name was likely chosen to describe white talcum powder. These days talcum powder is used for cosmetic and baby products, as it leaves a very silky feel. Talc is also used as a lubricant and as a filler in paint, rubber, and paper.

As soapstone is heated, it becomes extremely hard. Inuit made good use of this material for oil lamps and stoves. Some modern wood stoves are also made of soapstone for this reason.

Silicates

Tourmaline

Silicate – Tourmaline –
$(Ca,Na,K)(Al,Fe^{2+},Fe^{3+},Li,Mg,Mn)_3(Al,Cr,Fe^{3+},V^{3+})_6(BO_3)_3Si_6O_{18}(O,OH,F)_4$
Family and Crystal System: Silicate; trigonal (three out of four **axes** lie on the same plane, are of equal lengths, and intersect at 120°; fourth axis is not of the same length and not perpendicular)

Appearance

Tourmaline **crystals** are common and usually **prismatic**. Sometimes the end sections are triangular and display rounded faces. The two ends of the prisms have different sets of faces. **Striations** quite commonly run lengthwise along the crystal sides. More rarely, tourmaline occurs in masses or **columnar** bundles or **radiating aggregates**.

Some interesting colour **zonation** can occur in tourmaline. Zonation occurs when there are colour changes occurring in bands. Crystals may fade from one colour to another lengthwise, along the prism. When looking directly at the end of the prism, **concentric** zones of colour may be seen.

Tourmaline is usually black, but almost any colour can be observed. It has a **vitreous lustre** and is **translucent** to transparent.

Physical Properties

The mineral does not break easily into regular shapes and so does not have a **cleavage**. If fractured, the pattern is uneven or **conchoidal**. It is quite hard, at 7 to 7.5 on the **Mohs scale** and it has a **specific gravity** of 3 to 3.2.

Photo: Royal Ontario Museum

Environment & Occurrence

Tourmaline is actually a whole group of minerals. Based on the complex formula, many different variants are possible. Tourmaline is most commonly found in granite pegmatite. In addition, it can form in some **igneous** and **metamorphic** rocks. Dravite, a brown tourmaline, can be found in metamorphosed limestones. The black tourmaline is frequently found in quartz **veins**.

Photo: Danny Christopher

Approximately 350 kilometres east of Hall Beach, and in the centre of Baffin Island, is a pegmatite locality known for its huge tourmaline crystals. Some of the crystals measure up to 1 metre long, with a diameter of 1.25 centimetres. It also occurs as **dendritic** aggregates.

Did You Know?

Tourmaline is one of the most popular **gemstones** due to its abundance of lovely colours. The black tourmaline is called schorl. Pink to red tourmaline is rubellite. Blue variants are called indicolite and green crystals are elbaite. When the zonation is concentric, the stone is called watermelon tourmaline, because the green rind and pink centre looks very much like the fruit.

Silicates

Tremolite

Silicate – Tremolite – $Ca_2(Mg,Fe^{2+})_5Si_8O_{22}(OH)_2$
Alternate Names: Asbestos; nephrite; jade; grammatite
Family and Crystal System: Silicate; amphibole group; monoclinic
(three **axes** all of different lengths; two axes at right angles; third axis inclined)

Appearance

Tremolite **crystals** are usually long, skinny rods and can be arranged in a fan shape or as a bundle of parallel crystals. Sometimes the crystals are so narrow they are called **fibrous**. Tremolite can also occur in **massive** lumps in which the crystals are not easily seen.

A small range of colours is exhibited by this mineral, from white to grey. The crystal's **lustre** is **vitreous**, so it looks a lot like glass when the light shines on it. Normally the grains are **translucent** to transparent.

Photo: Danny Christopher

Physical Properties

Tremolite is ranked 5.5 to 6 on the **Mohs scale**. Its **specific gravity** is 3 to 3.4 and tremolite has two **perfect cleavages**, which form an angle of 56° to one another.

Environment & Occurrence

Tremolite can be found in **metamorphic** rocks as well as in its related partner mineral, actinolite. Tremolite is formed through many stages of **metamorphism** (changes or alterations in a rock), and is also found in limestones that contain some magnesium (dolomitic limestones). Kimmirut marble also contains tremolite.

In contact metamorphic rocks (rocks that are changed because of heat from a hot **magma** body), tremolite is found with garnet and calcite. Tremolite forms in serpentinites, alongside talc, and even in some **igneous** rocks, where it is an **alteration product** of pyroxene. Alteration happens when a mineral changes to something else because of the presence of a hot fluid, or the action of **weathering**.

Tremolite in tough and compact masses is called nephrite and is sometimes referred to as jade. It is good for carving, and making jewellery and ornaments.

The hairy form of tremolite is called asbestos and it was used extensively in the past to make insulation for buildings. Asbestos is still used to make fireproof fabrics and electrical insulators.

Photo: Royal Ontario Museum

Silicates

Rock
Descriptions

Andesite

Igneous – Extrusive – Andesite

Field Features

Andesite is a tough rock that resists **weathering** and **erosion**, so it is usually well exposed in **outcrops** (**bedrock** that sticks up through the overlying cover of **glacial debris**) and is associated with other **volcanic** rocks. If it cooled very quickly from the **molten** state, sometimes a series of cracks will have developed, giving the outcrop a **platy** appearance.

Textures

Andesite is a fine-grained rock, which may have occasional coarser grains (causing what is known as a **porphyritic** texture). The larger plagioclase grains are commonly white, giving the rock a spotted look. Other minerals may also form the larger grains instead of plagioclase. For instance, it could be replaced by pyroxene, biotite mica, or hornblende.

Physical Description

Andesite is normally a medium-toned colour. Green and grey are common, but brown, purple, and near black are also observed.

Mineral Constituents

Plagioclase, pyroxene, amphibole, and biotite mica are the common constituents. Quartz, olivine, or orthoclase may be present in small amounts.

Environment

Andesite is a rock that forms from **lava**, which flows out of a volcano. It is usually associated with volcanoes that sit above a **subduction zone**, a place on the Earth's **crust** where two crustal plates collide and the oceanic plate bends down to pass under the **continental plate**. Andesite may also form in a **dike**.

At Izok Lake, in the southwestern part of the Kitikmeot region, two larger andesite **units** are found over wide areas. The Lower Andesite is located 3 kilometres west of

Izok Lake and is a **deformed** rock unit. There is an Upper Andesite as well, immediately east of Izok Lake, which contains some quartz-filled **gas** bubbles.

Traditional & Modern Uses

Andesite is sometimes used for building stone.

Did You Know?

Andesite has been produced in large quantities from the volcanoes found in the Andes mountain chain of western South America. The name for the rock is derived from this location. Large copper **deposits** are often found in andesite rocks.

Photo: Danny Christopher

Igneous Extrusive

Ash Tuff

Igneous – Extrusive – Ash Tuff

Field Features

Ash tuffs are soft rocks and therefore tend not to be well exposed, since they break down quite easily. Ash tuff layers are usually found interspersed with **massive volcanic flow rocks**.

Textures

Ash tuffs can be layered or massive. Because the fragments fall through the air and possibly through water, they can form structures that resemble **sedimentary** features (like bedding or layers).

Sometimes spherical or oval balls, called lapilli, can be found in ash tuff. They are formed from the repeated **deposition** of more **ash** around the initial piece of ash that flew out of the volcano, forming **concentric** layers. As with the development of hail, lapilli require winds or air currents to carry the ash fragments repeatedly up and down in a cycle along the alternating air currents. Each time the ash fragment passes near the volcanic **vent**, it grows some more.

Physical Description

When massive, ash tuffs have randomly scattered fragments of **lava** or **crystals**. The resulting rock is fine- to medium-grained and spotty. Medium-toned colours are common, such as brown and grey. Pink, yellow, and white are much more rare. When crystals are scattered throughout, they are usually very good quality. Ash tuffs generally have a rough, gritty feel. They can always be scratched with a knife.

Mineral Constituents

Tuff is the general name for this rock. Ash tuff, made from very tiny volcanic rock pieces, is the most common type of tuff. If ash fragments combine with larger rock fragments of the lava, whether rhyolite, andesite, or trachyte, it is called lithic tuff.

In the formation of crystal tuff, which takes place during a volcanic eruption, new crystals form and are blown out of the volcano along with the ash. The crystals are usually feldspars, pyroxenes, and amphiboles. Glass or pumice fragments are also commonly observed in tuff.

Photo: Danny Christopher

Environment

Ash tuff forms from volcanic ash that is blown up into the atmosphere. If the eruption is very explosive, the ash may travel many miles through the upper atmosphere. Winds will then carry the ash a long way. As the sun sets through these high ash clouds, it can create beautiful sunsets. If the ash falls into a lake or sea, the water body may become layered.

Along the Back River in the central Kitikmeot region, there is a relatively undeformed volcano, which geologists have named the Back River volcanic **complex**. It has several ash tuff layers intermixed with flows (a body of rock formed by a single outpouring of lava through the feeder zone) of andesite, dacite, and rhyolite. On the north side of this volcano, the ash tuff and flows were deposited in a shallow marine environment. This volcano was active 2.7 billion years ago and is now dead.

Traditional & Modern Uses

One of the modern uses for ash tuff is construction material. It is also an ingredient in special cements.

Did You Know?

Blocks or **bombs** may also be found in the tuff. Blocks are large angular chunks of rock that were ripped up from solidified lava or from rocks next to volcanic vents. When larger blocks and fragments are formed through the explosive activity of a volcano, the rock is called **agglomerate**.

Bombs are rounded chunks of **molten** lava that solidify as they fly through the air. Generally bombs are hard and solid by the time they hit the ground. Large-scale features like blocks and bombs are good indicators of proximity to a volcanic vent.

Igneous Extrusive

Basalt

Igneous – Extrusive – Basalt

Field Features

Basalt **outcrops** (**bedrock** that sticks up through the overlying cover of **glacial debris**) may be extensive and show some variations from one layer to another. In some cases, an interesting pattern of cracks may form, called **columnar jointing**. Six-sided columns are topped with flat surfaces and erode to different heights, creating a steplike exposure.

Textures

A **massive** basalt is a fine-grained rock and its individual **crystals** cannot be seen clearly with the naked eye. **Porphyritic** basalt contains some larger crystals spotted throughout an otherwise massive rock. The larger grains can be either olivine, pyroxene, or plagioclase.

Physical Description

Typically black, basalts can also be brownish or greyish. Sometimes they will weather, forming a green or red **crust** (thin layer or coating). **Gas** bubbles (empty or filled by late minerals created after the original basalt) may be present. A striking form of basalt is called pillowed basalt, due to pillow shapes seen in outcrops. The pillows form when **lava** flows into water and the outer surface chills very rapidly, forming a skinlike layer.

Mineral Constituents

The principal minerals in basalt are plagioclase and pyroxene. Apatite and magnetite are generally also present, but in small amounts. Hornblende and olivine may also be present.

Environment

Basalt is the most common rock formed from **volcanic lava**. In the ancient regions of Nunavut, in greenstone belts, the most common rock found is basalt. It is commonly green when metamorphosed, that is, affected by changes in temperature and/or pressure. Basalts are formed from a thin, runny lava, the resulting flows of which form extensive

Photo: Danny Christopher

sheets on the flanks of volcanoes and on the valley floors. Most of the sea floor is made of basalt. The basalt was **extruded** at long mid-**oceanic ridges** (places at the edges of oceanic crust where new rocks are formed through volcanic activity). In Iceland, the mid-oceanic ridge is actually up on the land and is therefore accessible to geologists. Rather than volcanic cones and craters, this type of volcanism occurs along long cracks in the crust, which can go on for kilometres. The **magma** seeps out of the cracks and will sometimes fountain up, creating a spectacular display.

Basalt may also flow through and solidify within a fracture in the crust, forming a **dike**.

In the Meadowbank mine area, basalts occur with **ultramafic** rock exposures. Basalts can also be seen on Goose Island. There, the basalt has larger crystals of plagioclase and sometimes pyroxene, set in a **matrix** (the finer-grained material in a rock that surrounds any coarser-grained minerals) that also contains abundant chlorite.

Traditional & Modern Uses

Because basalt is a tough rock, it is often used for road paving and as railroad ballast; basalt can be used to cover the ground before the rails are laid down. Basalt can also be used over river banks to stabilize the shoreline where too much **erosion** has occurred. This material is called traprock. Basalt is sometimes used as a building stone, in the manufacture of rock wool (a type of insulation), and in fiberglass.

Did You Know?

Along the Columbia River in the western United States, basalts cover an impressive 500,000 square kilometres. The basalt flowed for so long that it accumulated to a thickness of over 3 kilometres.

Igneous Extrusive

Dacite

Igneous – Extrusive – Dacite

Field Features

Dacite is a tough, hard rock. Dacite will form resistant exposures, meaning that the **outcrops** will stick up higher than some other rocks in the area.

Textures

Dacite is either **massive** or **porphyritic**. Most of the minerals will be fine-grained. **Flow banding** may be observed, and if many large **crystals** are present, they too will be aligned with their long **axes** along the flow direction.

Physical Description

Rocks form due to specific chemical reactions. These reactions take place in an orderly fashion, with certain reactions happening before others. In a **magma** chamber (an underground reservoir), when rocks are being formed, iron- and magnesium-rich rocks form first, followed by intermediate rocks such as dacite. Dacite falls between rhyolite and andesite and as such, is light- to medium-coloured. The colour can be white, grey, buff, pale to deep red, brown, or, on rare occasions, black.

Mineral Constituents

The main minerals in dacite are quartz and plagioclase. Minor amounts of pyroxene, hornblende, and biotite will be found. Very small amounts of orthoclase, apatite, garnet, and magnetite may also be included. Some glass may also be observed.

Environment

Dacite is primarily found in small **lava flows**, but it may also solidify within cracks in the Earth and may form small **intrusions**.

Traditional & Modern Uses

Dacite is crushed and the loose pieces are used for road construction. It is also used as ornamental and decorative stone.

Did You Know?

Dacite is such a thick liquid (as a lava flow) that sometimes it can barely move. Instead the dacite grows upward, forming a **dome** of rocks. In some places this growth happens so slowly that people can safely walk over the top of the volcano dome.

Photo: Shutterstone.com

Igneous Extrusive

Obsidian

Igneous – Extrusive – Obsidian

Field Features

Obsidian is a glassy and uniform-looking rock.

Textures

Obsidian is so fine-grained that it is completely glassy. It may contain larger quartz and plagioclase grains visible to the naked eye. The rock fractures in a **conchoidal** pattern, which resembles a clamshell.

Physical Description

Obsidian is shiny black, brown, or grey. If it has small circular white patches, which resemble snowflakes, it is called snowflake obsidian. Once in a while, **flow banding** may be observed. **Gas** bubbles may also be seen and could contain other tiny **crystals**. Obsidian is a very hard rock.

Mineral Constituents

Obsidian is mostly composed of quartz but may also contain plagioclase.

Environment

Obsidian is formed by the exceedingly rapid cooling down of very thick **volcanic lava** that is full of silica. It can form as **dikes** or as flows (bodies of rock formed by a single outpouring of lava through the feeder zone). Because it is so hard, **outcrops** of obsidian generally stand up high. Obsidian is found close to rhyolite because these two minerals are chemically very similar.

Obsidian does not occur in large quantities and is very rare in Nunavut because over time the glass breaks down and changes to a white powdery rock. Because there aren't any active volcanoes in Nunavut, the likelihood of finding good-quality obsidian specimens is very low.

Since prehistoric times, humans have used this rock to make cutting tools. To make a tool, the obsidian is gradually chipped away with a razor-sharp edge, which results in two or more well-placed fractures. Knives, arrowheads, spear tips, and many other tools were made from obsidian in the past. These days, obsidian is used to manufacture rock wool, which is a type of insulation. It also polishes well and is often used as a semi-precious stone for jewellery making.

Did You Know?

On rare occasions, fragments of obsidian are thrown out of the **vent** of a volcano. Sometimes these fragments can be strandlike and are referred to as Pele's hair. Pele is a Hawaiian goddess of volcanoes. These light golden brown, hairlike obsidian fragments are extremely soft and flexible. Smart birds will even collect this material to line their nests!

Photo: Danny Christopher

Igneous Extrusive

Rhyolite

Igneous – Extrusive – Rhyolite

Field Features

Rhyolite is a hard rock and forms jagged **outcrops** that stand up high. Generally the rock is a very pale colour.

Textures

Rhyolite can be **massive**, **porphyritic**, or **flow banded**.

Physical Description

Usually the minerals are so fine-grained that they are not visible. Rhyolite is normally a

Photo: Danny Christopher

light colour—white, grey, green, red, or brown. It is a hard rock and **gas** bubbles can be seen preserved in the rock. Occasionally the bubbles become filled with a late mineral created after the original rhyolite, like quartz or feldspar (plagioclase or orthoclase).

Mineral Constituents

Quartz, orthoclase, plagioclase, and a small amount of biotite and hornblende are the common minerals found in rhyolite. Sometimes a little glass will be present as well.

Environment

Rhyolite forms during explosive **volcanic** eruptions. A very thick **lava** flows sluggishly out of the volcano, which cools and solidifies to form rhyolite. Sometimes the lava does not make it very far before **crystallizing**. In these cases, the lava forms **domes** and **dikes**.

At Izok Lake, near the Northwest Territories (NWT) boundary, rhyolite is an important rock type. Two main varieties can be observed there—one is **massive** and the other has larger quartz grains that are easy to see. There is also a very large massive sulphide **deposit** there, consisting of sphalerite, pyrite, and chalcopyrite, which is enveloped on both sides by rhyolite.

Traditional & Modern Uses

These days, rhyolite is used to make crushed rock for various building purposes and as a paving stone.

Did You Know?

Lava domes made of rhyolite sit inside the craters of modern day volcanoes. Volcanologists (scientists who study volcanoes) measure the height and width of these domes and watch for unusual growth. It is well known that a major eruption is usually signaled by rapid **dome** growth.

Anorthosite

Igneous – Intrusive – Anorthosite

Field Features

Very often anorthosite is interlayered with gabbro. It may form very large **intrusions**, or smaller **stocks** and **dikes**.

Textures

Usually this rock is **massive**, but on occasion there will be an alignment of long grains. Dark minerals may forms **streaks** along this same alignment.

Physical Description

This rock is grey to white. Minerals are medium- to coarse-grained and are scattered randomly throughout the rock.

Mineral Constituents

Anorthosite is made up almost entirely of plagioclase. Minor amounts of pyroxene, olivine, and magnetite may also be found.

Environment

Anorthosite solidifies from a **magma**. It is often formed as part of a layered **complex** along with gabbro.

On Hudson Bay, east of Baker Lake, the Daly Bay complex is a very large region of **intrusive rocks**. Anorthosite, containing pyroxene, is a major part of the outer edges of this complex. During a period of intense **regional metamorphism**, parts of the upper **mantle** melted, which created a magma that moved up into the lower **crust**. There the rock solidified, about two billion years ago.

Photo: Danny Christopher

Traditional & Modern Uses

Attractive anorthosite varieties are used for decorative purposes and for making jewellery. One type of plagioclase is blue with a lovely internal rainbow effect. If the anorthosite contains an abundance of this blue mineral, it is called labradorite. This beautiful rock is in high demand for countertops, jewellery, and for building stone.

Did You Know?

Some of the rocks collected from the surface of the moon are anorthosite.

Igneous Intrusive

Diabase

Igneous – Intrusive – Diabase

Field Features

Diabase will often resist **erosion** and form long ridges. It is not unusual to find several diabase **dikes** in the same vicinity, generally running in the same direction. Diabase often develops an orange to brown rind on its outer surface due to the rusting of sulphide minerals. Sometimes diabase will display a pattern of fractures that appear like columns packed tightly together. These columns can be quite regular in shape, and six-sided. These columns are usually 30 centimetres wide, but can be many metres high.

Textures

In some instances, there will be some grains that are much larger than others, which gives a random spotty texture to the diabase. On rare occasions you may find some crude layering, with coarser grains near one edge and finer grains toward the other side.

Physical Description

Generally black on fresh surfaces, diabase can also be dark grey or green. Very often it is mottled black and white. Minerals are typically medium-grained. Diabase is quite **magnetic**.

Mineral Constituents

The most common minerals in diabase are olivine, plagioclase, and pyroxene. In addition, there may be tiny grains of quartz, hornblende, or biotite. The magnetic minerals in diabase are magnetite or pyrrhotite.

Environment

Diabase solidifies from an underground **magma**. It forms in relatively narrow fractures in the **bedrock** and thus winds up forming dikes and **sills**. If the surrounding rocks could magically be stripped away, the diabase would look like a thin, flat sheet that extends for a great distance.

It is not unusual to find hundreds of diabase dikes in one area. Geologists refer to this as a **dike swarm**.

If you ever get a chance to visit the tiny community of Bathurst Inlet, take a hike up the huge ridge just south of town. It climbs to a height of about 400 metres and is made of diabase. Many traditional camping and hunting spots are found up on the ridge.

Traditional & Modern Uses

Diabase is a very tough rock and is well suited for use as a crushed rock for building materials, road metal (suitable for surfacing roads or for foundations for asphalt and concrete roadways), railroad ballast (diabase that can be used to cover the ground before the rails are laid down), roofing granules, and rip-rap. Rip-rap are large, angular blocks of rock that are used to build breakwaters or to stabilize the banks of rivers. Attractive varieties can be polished and used for cladding (a thin decorative outer layer) and are often misnamed black granite.

Did You Know?

Where diabase dikes are found to run in a radial pattern, like spokes in a wheel, they point inward to the magma chamber from which they were formed. This location will usually lie under a **volcanic** cone. A diabase is actually a basalt that never managed to make it to the surface.

In some old geology books you will find the word dolerite used instead of diabase.

Photo: Danny Christopher

Igneous Intrusive

Diorite

Igneous – Intrusive – Diorite

Field Features

Diorite can be found in **outcrops** that are a chemical mixture between granite and gabbro. Diorite will also form large outcrop areas on its own. Diorite forms **stocks** (small **intrusions**), **dikes**, and **sills**. Outcrops tend to be broad and **dome**-shaped, but not as high as granite hills. Diorite surfaces may show signs of **weathering**, like pitting (small, circular indentations on the surface) or gouging (long and narrow indentations).

Textures

Usually diorite is coarse-grained and the minerals are clearly identifiable. The grains may be randomly distributed and all about the same size (a **granular** texture), although some grains may be quite a bit larger than others (**porphyritic** texture).

Physical Description

This rock is generally quite speckled in appearance, normally black and white. Alternatively, the colour may be dark green or pink.

Mineral Constituents

Key minerals include plagioclase and hornblende. Biotite and pyroxene may be found. In some instances, quartz and orthoclase will also be found, especially where diorite is chemically similar in composition to granodiorite.

Environment

As with all **intrusive rocks**, diorite solidified from a **magma** while in the Earth's **crust**. Diomite collected in a magma chamber (an underground reservoir) and cooled down very slowly, over hundreds or thousands of years. It is not a very common rock.

Approximately 18 kilometres west of the Lupin mine site, there is a diorite **pluton**. This large diorite body of rock is situated on the south edge of a large area of granodiorite.

Photo: Danny Christopher

Traditional & Modern Uses

Cobblestones are made from diorite, as are other building stones. Crushed diorite is used for road building.

Did You Know?

Around the edges of a diorite body it is common to find xenoliths. These are blocks of a foreign rock, which were engulfed by the diorite magma and then eventually locked into place in the solidified rock.

Igneous *Intrusive*

Gabbro

Igneous – Intrusive – Gabbro

Field Features

Gabbro will form in **stocks**, **sills**, and **dikes**—all places where the **magma**, a hot fluid, solidified slowly in the Earth's **crust**. Sometimes large **intrusions**, up to several kilometres, may result. The rock is softer than granite and so it will form small hills. The surface is often covered by crumbly and broken bits of gabbro. Many of the minerals rust when exposed to air, so the surface may be a distinct reddish brown, rusty colour.

Textures

A layering of different minerals may be evident in gabbro. Towards the bottom of a layer, there are more dark-coloured minerals, and towards the top, it becomes light-coloured. Some gabbros are **massive** and do not have any layering at all. **Crystals** are very tightly intermeshed, which makes it a tough rock.

Physical Description

Normally the texture of gabbro is **granular**, consisting of grains about the same size. The grains are coarse to very large (called pegmatite). Gabbro is dark grey or black and may sometimes have a greenish or bluish tint. Even when very dark, gabbro often has a speckled appearance.

Photo: Danny Christopher

146

Mineral Constituents

Plagioclase and pyroxene are the essential minerals in gabbro. You may see quartz, olivine, or hornblende, as well as the accessory minerals magnetite, hematite, chromite, and serpentine.

Environment

Gabbro solidifies underground in magma chambers (underground reservoirs) and in various cracks. Occasionally gabbro will form a mushroom-shaped body, with layered rocks in the top portion. This type of layering is termed a **lopolith** and can be very extensive, attaining a diameter of several kilometres.

A good example of a large lopolith is the Muskox intrusion, which is south of Kugluktuk. The upper portions of this body are gabbro and olivine gabbro. Broad layers sweep across the upper funnel-shaped part of this intrusion.

Traditional & Modern Uses

Gabbro is often used for building and ornamental stone. It is also used for railway ballast (gabbro is used to cover the ground before the rails are laid down), because it is very tough and dense.

Did You Know?

This rock got its name from a town in the Tuscany region of Italy, which comes from the Latin word *glaber*, meaning smooth.

Igneous Intrusive

Granite

Igneous – Intrusive – Granite

Field Features

Large **outcrop** areas consist of granite. Due to a great uniformity of textures in all directions, and the hard nature of this rock, outcrops tend to be rounded off and form high hills.

Textures

The texture is usually consistent over very large areas. The predominant observation is that the rock is **granular**, which means that it consists of grains that are about the same size and usually equal in width and length. Occasionally some grains will be quite a bit larger than others and, if scattered throughout the rock, this is called a **porphyritic** texture.

Photo: Royal Ontario Museum

Physical Description

Typically granite is white, light grey, pink, red, or light, mottled shades of these colours. Individual grains are visible and can usually be identified with the naked eye. Coarse-grained rocks contain large grains.

Mineral Constituents

Orthoclase is the most common mineral found in granite. There may be large amounts of plagioclase as well. Quartz is also found in significant amounts. Beyond these key minerals, biotite, hornblende, or magnetite may be found. Other interesting minerals will occur in tiny amounts, like apatite, zircon, and sphene.

Environment

Granite occurs in large **intrusive** bodies called **batholiths**, or in **stocks**, **sills**, and **dikes**. At its **contacts** (or edges) granite can be seen to cross-cut other earlier formed rocks.

In regions with **metamorphic** rocks, the granite may be seen to transition gradually from a granular granite to a **banded** rock known as gneiss.

Granite is a common rock. Many examples of it can be found in the glacial **till** that covers Nunavut. Till **deposits** are the loose cobbles and boulders left lying around by the last glaciers that crossed the land. Because granite is so tough, it generally survives the transport abuse inflicted either within or underneath a glacier. This toughness is why so many of the cobbles are granite.

Traditional & Modern Uses

For a long time, granite has been used as a building stone. Due to its high quartz content, which makes the rock tough, it stands up well to wear and tear. It is also often used as road fill. As Inuit carvers know, granite is beautiful for sculptural work, but very difficult to work with due to its **hardness**.

Did You Know?

The "granite" countertops popular in today's modern kitchens aren't always granite. In the building stone industry, almost any rock with shiny flecks is called granite but, in fact, may not be granite at all.

Photo: Danny Christopher

Igneous Intrusive

Granodiorite

Igneous – Intrusive – Granodiorite

Field Features

These very common rocks are quite similar to granite and occur in large **outcrop** areas. Smooth, rounded off, domelike hills are common.

Textures

The rock is generally medium to coarse-grained and minerals can be identified with the naked eye. Granodiorite is **granular**, which means that most grains are evenly distributed throughout the rock and individual mineral grains are roughly as long as they are wide.

Physical Description

Light grey is the most common colour in granodiorite, but pink and red can also occur.

Mineral Constituents

Much like granite, the main mineral is plagioclase, followed by orthoclase, and quartz. Lesser amounts of biotite and hornblende are generally found.

Environment

Batholiths (very large **igneous intrusions** that can go deep in the Earth's **crust**), **stocks**, **dikes**, and **sills** are all possible formations for bodies of granodiorite. This rock solidifies from **magma** in chambers or cracks underground.

Around Iqaluit, many of the hills are composed of granodiorite and granodiorite gneiss. The latter is a **metamorphic** rock and it displays a clear separation of light- and dark-coloured minerals. The granodiorite will have an even mixing of the feldspars (plagioclase and orthoclase) with all other minerals. The main desk of the lobby of the Government of Canada building in Iqaluit is made of polished granodiorite.

Traditional & Modern Uses

This rock is often used for ornamental and building stone.

Did You Know?

Granodiorite is a transitional rock; it is between granite and diorite, as its name suggests. Rocks are usually, at least in part, mixtures of two different rock types. Granodiorite is possibly the most common intrusive igneous rock in the world!

Photo: Danny Christopher

Igneous *Intrusive*

Igneous Rocks - Intrusive
Kimberlite

Igneous – Intrusive – Kimberlite

Field Features

Kimberlite bodies are generally oval or round. They are not very large, usually not more than 300 metres across. The rock itself is soft and susceptible to **erosion** and so small lakes and ponds sometimes cover kimberlite exposures.

Photo: Royal Ontario Museum

Textures

The grains in kimberlite are randomly jumbled, so there may be large fragments of other rocks locked into the kimberlite.

Physical Description

Kimberlite is most commonly greenish, bluish, or black, but it may be any colour. The grains are typically coarse and often the larger grains have rounded edges. The rock may look spotty, with some larger minerals creating the appearance of a mottled texture, which is called a **porphyritic** texture.

Mineral Constituents

The most common minerals found in kimberlite include olivine, phlogopite, and garnet. The olivine is generally changed to serpentine. Pyroxene, especially a bright green diopside variety, is also observed. In much smaller quantities, there will be some ilmenite, chromite, and, rarely, diamond. Calcite can be abundant.

152

Environment

Kimberlite rises very rapidly through a **volcanic pipe** (a cylindrical **intrusion** of rock), which often erupts explosively at the Earth's surface. The shape of the kimberlite body is like a pipe or a carrot steeply dipping into the crust of the Earth. Sometimes kimberlite **magma** will follow a fracture and then the resulting body of rock is a **dike**. As the magma rises violently up through the crust, it rips chunks off nearby rocks and carries them up towards the surface. These **blocks** often get trapped into the kimberlite rock and indicate what types of rocks lie deep in the crust.

Just 120 kilometres southwest of Kugaaruk, there are several kimberlites on the Darby project. These kimberlites contain very large grains in a medium to coarse **matrix** (the finer-grained material in a rock that surrounds any coarser-grained mineral). Phlogopite and calcite are key minerals in these rocks.

Traditional & Modern Uses

Kimberlite is an important source of diamonds. When diamonds are not of good quality, they are used for many industrial applications, like abrasives.

Did You Know?

When exploring for diamond **occurrences** in Nunavut, geologists study the loose boulders and cobbles that are strewn about the land. During the last ice age, when huge ice sheets advanced over the land, this ice scoured the soft kimberlite and spread it in a single direction—the same direction in which the ice was moving. By mapping the location of the kimberlite boulders, a line can be drawn back to the source area and hopefully the location of kimberlite exposures in the **bedrock**.

Igneous Intrusive

Lamprophyre

Igneous – Intrusive – Lamprophyre

Field Features

Lamprophyre is commonly found near granite, syenite, and diorite. Look for it in the **margin zones** (the area around the edges of an **intrusion**) of these intrusions. It will commonly form narrow **dikes**, less than a metre wide.

Textures

Normally lamprophyre has some dark-coloured grains which are quite a bit larger than its other grains. This texture is called **porphyritic**.

Physical Description

Grey, black, or green lamprophyre eventually weathers to a red or brown colour. Grains are generally medium to fine-grained. Only some minerals are identifiable with the naked eye.

Mineral Constituents

There are two main types of lamprophyre: one type has large biotite grains scattered throughout and the second has hornblende grains. In both cases, the same mineral will also occur in the finer-grained material. In addition, there will be fine orthoclase or plagioclase, and perhaps pyroxene. The biotite-rich variety is also rich in calcite, so a drop of hydrochloric acid on this rock will produce a strong fizzing reaction. This variety will feel soft when struck with a hammer.

Environment

Lamprophyre forms small intrusive bodies like dikes, **sills**, and small **plugs**.

On rare occasions, lamprophyre may contain micro diamonds, which are very tiny diamonds. One example is the biotite-rich lamprophyre between Rankin Inlet and Baker Lake, called the Parker Lake dike. In a 22-kilogram sample taken from this lamprophyre, over 1,500 micro diamonds were found.

Traditional & Modern Uses

There is no commercial value in this rock. Sometimes, rocks have no practical uses but geologists still give them names and describe their properties, as is the case with lamprophyre.

Did You Know?

Minette is a lamprophyre associated with syenites. It contains pyroxene, biotite, and orthoclase. Spessartite is a lamprophyre associated with diorite. It contains more plagioclase, hornblende, and pyroxene.

Photo: Shutterstone.com

Igneous Intrusive

Monzonite

Igneous – Intrusive – Monzonite

Field Features

Monzonite tends to form smaller **outcrops**. It can be closely related to areas of granite and granodiorite.

Textures

This rock is usually medium-grained. Most minerals within monzonite will be identifiable with the naked eye. The minerals are generally randomly distributed in the rock, but sometimes an alignment of longer **crystals**, which indicates a flow direction from the time the **magma** was still liquid, can be seen.

Physical Description

Monzonite is typically light to dark grey, but it can also be green, brown, or red.

Photo: Danny Christopher

Mineral Constituents

In monzonite, expect to see nearly equal proportions of orthoclase and plagioclase. Usually very little quartz is present and it may sometimes be absent altogether. In some rare cases, nepheline will occur in monzonite. Pyroxene may be present in significant quantities. Hornblende and biotite are other dark minerals that may be present.

Environment

A monzonite body forms in the same way as granite, by slow cooling of magma deep in the Earth's **crust**.

Just northwest of Rankin Inlet and a little west of the West Meliadine gold **deposits**, is the Peter Lake area, where **metamorphosed volcanic** and **sedimentary** rocks can be found. Formed at a later time, there is a monzonite **stock**, which intrudes into the earlier rocks. From the way the **contacts** meet in that area, it is clear that the monzonite has disrupted the sequence of the earlier formed rocks.

Traditional & Modern Uses

Monzonite is an attractive rock and is used for building stone and ornamental work.

Did You Know?

Monzonite is a transitional rock, in both chemistry and mineralogy, between the syenite and diorite types.

Igneous Intrusive

Nepheline Syenite

Igneous – Intrusive – Nepheline Syenite

Field Features

Nepheline syenite is a rare rock. It forms **stocks**, **dikes**, and **sills**.

Textures

Nepheline syenite contains grains that are all square or round, and normally about the same size. Sometimes it will display some larger grains scattered throughout the smaller grains. On rare occasions, some rectangular grains will run all the same way, which indicates the flow of the **magma** while the rock was still **molten**.

Physical Description

This rock is usually grey, but it may have tones of yellow, pink, or green. Grains are generally coarse or even giant-sized. Nepheline is a greasy and waxy-looking mineral.

Mineral Constituents

The main minerals are orthoclase, plagioclase, nepheline, pyroxene, hornblende, or biotite. A blue mineral, sodalite, or a yellow or orange mineral, cancrinite, may also be found.

Environment

As an **intrusive rock**, nepheline syenite cools and **crystallizes** underground. It forms medium to small **intrusions**. It may form in an area with other unusual rocks that are rich in sodium and potassium elements. These may be varieties of gabbro and granite.

Traditional & Modern Uses

Nepheline syenite is used as a building and ornamental stone. It is also used in road building. Sometimes this rock is mined to extract the sodium, aluminum, and potassium from the minerals for use in the chemical industry. The ceramics industry also uses nepheline syenite.

Nepheline and pectolite are reported from an area known as Napoleon Bay on Baffin Island. These two minerals occur in nepheline syenite. Also, at Kimmirut, there are localities with nepheline and hauyne, another mineral usually found in nepheline syenite.

Did You Know?

The mineral quartz will never be found in nepheline syenite because the chemistry of the original magma is not rich enough in silica to allow quartz to form. Though nepheline can look similar to quartz, nepheline can be scratched with a pocket knife, while quartz is harder than the metal in a knife blade.

Photo: Shutterstone.com

Igneous Intrusive

Pegmatite

Igneous – Intrusive – Pegmatite

Field Features

Pegmatite is often associated with granite and contains the same minerals. Around the outside of a granite **intrusion**, a **margin zone** of pegmatite may be found. **Dikes** of pegmatite will also be found intruding through the country rock, which is the pre-existing rock all around the intrusion.

Textures

The **crystals** in a pegmatite often grow at 90° to the outer wall of the intrusion. Narrow **veins** and small dikes are common forms for pegmatite intrusions. In some pegmatite veins, there are open cavities with large crystals arranged all around the rim.

Physical Description

Pegmatites are the most coarse-grained rocks, with some crystals reaching over 10 metres in size. White, pink, and red are the most common colours but the rock is blotchy due to the very large grain size. Most of the grains will have perfectly developed crystal forms.

Photo: Danny Christopher

Mineral Constituents

The minerals in pegmatite are much the same as those in granite: orthoclase, quartz, and muscovite. Other minerals that may be found are biotite, plagioclase, tourmaline, fluorite, pyrite, and chalcopyrite.

Environment

Pegmatites take shape after the bulk of a granite intrusion has already formed. The last remaining **magma** and hot **gases** have all sorts of odd chemicals, so the minerals that

crystallize are sometimes unusual and very rare. The last bit of magma cools very slowly, which allows for giant crystals to form.

Just as there is an association of granite with pegmatite, there is also a similar link between nepheline syenite and pegmatite. Thus the minerals in a nepheline syenite will also be found in the pegmatites nearby.

At Izok Lake, just along the Nunavut– Northwest Territories boundary in the Kitikmeot region, there are many granitic pegmatite dikes. These dikes appear to be associated with a granite intrusion about three kilometres west of Izok Lake. The irregular dikes contain quartz, orthoclase, muscovite, tourmaline, galena, and sphalerite.

Photo: Royal Ontario Museum

Traditional & Modern Uses

Pegmatites are sometimes mined for the highly rare and unusual minerals they contain. Lepidolite, for example, is a purple mica mineral, related to phlogopite and muscovite. Lepidolite is mined for the lithium it contains, which is used to make special **alloys**, lubricants, and for the manufacture of nuclear energy. Beryl is found in pegmatites and it is used to harden copper alloys.

Did You Know?

Pegmatites are ideal collectibles for the mineral and gem collector because the crystals are so large and well-formed that they are easy to identify. Also, valuable gems may be found in pegmatite, such as topaz, beryl, tourmaline, and kunzite.

It is important to be very careful when hammering on an **outcrop** of pegmatite, as hard hammering can easily damage some large and spectacular crystals. A good chisel and safety glasses are useful tools for gently prying out the better specimens.

Igneous Intrusive

Peridotite

Igneous – Intrusive – Peridotite

Field Features

Peridotite exposures may be found close to gabbro **outcrops**, as the rock type sometimes transitions from one to the other. Due to many minerals that rust and crumble at the Earth's surface, look for low, rounded hills with a medium to dark brown, pitted, and crumbly surface.

Textures

This rock has a **granular** texture in which minerals are evenly scattered throughout and all the grains are approximately round. In the dunite variety the texture is sugary. Sometimes a mineral layering can be seen in the outcrops.

Physical Description

Peridotite is an unremarkable rock, coloured dull green to black. In the dunite variety (made almost entirely of olivine), the colour is light to dark green shades, brown, and yellow. Grains are a medium to coarse size.

Photo: Danny Christopher

Mineral Constituents

Peridotite is mostly olivine, with lesser amounts of pyroxene and/or hornblende. If the rock is almost entirely olivine, it is called a dunite. Plagioclase is normally absent or occurring in very tiny amounts. Small amounts of biotite, chromite, or garnet may also be found.

Environment

Peridotite is usually formed within part of a larger **magma** chamber, an underground reservoir of **molten** rock. Heavy **crystals** of olivine sink to the bottom of the chamber, forming the layers, which eventually harden to become peridotite. In the same chamber, there may be areas that eventually form pyroxenite or gabbro.

The shapes of the resulting bodies include **dikes**, **sills**, and small **stocks**.

In Nunavut, the most extensive peridotites are in the Muskox **intrusion**, south of Kugluktuk. For many tens of kilometres, peridotite is interlayered with gabbro. This layering can be observed from an aircraft.

Traditional & Modern Uses

In peridotite, there can be several different kinds of minerals that may be worth mining, as nickel, chromite, and platinum can be found. Even diamonds come from a mica peridotite better known as kimberlite. The minerals talc and asbestos also come from this rock type. The olivine may be used in jewellery if grains are large, clear, and of good colour. Olivine is then called peridot (hence the name peridotite).

Did You Know?

When a peridotite rock is altered, some of the minerals convert to serpentine and talc. This is the material that carvers are always on the lookout for.

Igneous Intrusive

Syenite

Igneous – Intrusive – Syenite

Field Features

Syenite is not a very common rock, but it forms **outcrops**, much like granite. Syenite often forms rounded **domes**, which in turn creates hills. Sometimes granite will transition into syenite in the same area.

Textures

Most of the mineral grains will be roughly the same width and length, which makes for a **granular** rock. Sometimes there are isolated, larger grains scattered throughout, in which case the rock is **porphyritic**. Occasionally there may be a distinct preferred orientation in some rectangular grains, and they all line up along **magma** flow lines.

Physical Description

Syenite is coloured red, pink, grey, or white. In rare instances it is blue, green, purple, brown, yellow, or black.

Minerals in a syenite are usually coarse-grained and can be identified with the naked eye. Pegmatitic (very coarse-grained) minerals can also be observed.

Mineral Constituents

The predominant mineral in a syenite is orthoclase. Also found is plagioclase, quartz, and lesser quantities of biotite, amphibole, and pyroxene. Nepheline is a grey, waxy mineral that may be found in syenite, in which case quartz will not be present. If you find any quartz, you will not find nepheline, as the two minerals are mutually exclusive.

Environment

Syenite bodies may be **stocks** up to several kilometres wide. Syenite also forms **dikes** and **sills**. Often, another **igneous** rock called gabbro can occur with syenite.

Syenite occurs a few kilometres east of Ferguson Lake in the Uligataalik Hill area, due west of Rankin Inlet. This syenite transitions into granite and pegamatite, with very large **crystals** of feldspar.

Traditional & Modern Uses

As with granite, syenite is tough and takes a good polish, and is used for ornamental applications. Countertops, building stone, gravestones, and floor slabs are just a few of its uses. Nepheline syenite bodies are used for ceramic production, and very white nepheline syenites can be used for glass making.

Did You Know?

The name syenite comes from the place where it was first described: Syene, Egypt (now called Aswan). According to the way geologists now define rock types, the rock at Aswan would no longer be called syenite, but would be identified as granodiorite.

Photo: Danny Christopher

Igneous Intrusive

Dolostone

Sedimentary – Biogenic – Dolostone

Field Features

In **outcrops**, the dolostone will appear much like limestone and will weather in a similar way.

Textures

This rock has a crystalline (composed of **crystals**) texture and some of the individual crystals of dolomite that make up the rock can be seen. When the rock is more **massive**, it will appear dense and earthy.

Physical Description

Dolostone is typically a creamy brown colour, but it can also be light grey to tan. When compared to limestone, dolostone will have fewer **fossils**. Dolomite usually will not fizz when hydrochloric acid is poured on it. Occasionally, the rock will give off a rotten smell when hit with a hammer.

Photo: Danny Christopher

Mineral Constituents

Dolostone is made up mostly of dolomite, with some calcite. Small amounts of feldspars (plagioclase or orthoclase), quartz, and chert may also be found.

Environment

Dolostone is formed in a marine environment. It is thought that most dolostones are formed from limestones. The calcite in the limestones is replaced by dolomite as watery fluid percolates through the limestone, and creates the chemical changes.

Dolostone is also found interbedded with limestone near salt and gypsum **deposits**. Dolostone is an important host to **petroleum** deposits.

At the now-closed Nanisivik mine near Arctic Bay, dolostone was the host rock to the main ore zones of lead, zinc, and silver. These minerals were mined for many years at the Nanisivik mine. Great specimens of pyrite and dolomite were also found.

Traditional & Modern Uses

There are many industrial uses of dolostone. It goes into the manufacture of asphalt filler, concrete aggregate (crushed stone), rip-rap (construction stone), and roofing granules. As with limestone, it is used in the steel-making industry as a flux, which helps to speed up other chemical reactions. Dolostone is also a source of the pure metal magnesium, which can be used in vitamins and medicines.

Did You Know?

Some older reference books referred to a rock made mostly of the mineral dolomite, as a dolomite. Because these two different materials had the same name, there was cause for confusion, so most people now call the rock "dolostone" and the mineral "dolomite."

Sedimentary Biogenic

Chert

Sedimentary – Chemical – Chert

Field Features

Chert is usually found as **nodules** or in thin sheets in limestone or in **lava**. It is uncommon to find large quantities of chert. This rock is so tough and resistant to **erosion** that it stands out in relief in an **outcrop**. Even individual balls of chert will be noticeable.

Photo: Royal Ontario Museum

Textures

Chert is a **granular** rock, but the grains are so tiny they can only be seen with a microscope. Even with a microscope, they may be too small to be easily viewed. This kind of texture is called cryptocrystalline.

Physical Description

Chert is often grey but may range from white to almost black. Black varieties made of pure silica are called flint. Chert will less commonly be yellow, brown, green, or red. Red varieties are called jasper. This rock is very hard and cannot be scratched with a knife. If chipped, it will display an uneven to **conchoidal** fracture.

Mineral Constituents

Silica is the main constituent of chert, but some impurities such as clay minerals, calcite, or hematite may be found.

Environment

Silica collects on the sea floor and forms a gel-like substance, which eventually hardens to form chert. The actual source of the silica may be dead organisms (algae and protozoans), or liquids spewing out of hot springs in the sea floor, or sometimes the sea water itself. Chert is considered a chemical **sediment**.

Chert nodules are sometimes found in limestone. Small areas of the limestone are dissolved and replaced by chert, which is brought to the location by percolating silica-rich fluids.

The Polaris mine on Little Cornwallis Island was located in rocks called the Thumb Mountain formation. At the base of this group of rocks is a chert that measures 4 to 10 metres thick. While **weathering**, animal burrow channels are also evident in this chert. In rocks that were formed after the Thumb Mountain formation, there is more chert associated with shale and limestone.

Traditional & Modern Uses

Traditionally, chert was used to make weapons, common tools, and fire-starting tools. Early flintlock rifles used flint (very closely related to chert) to ignite the charge.

Did You Know?

While most rocks are made of a variety of different minerals, some rocks are made up entirely of one mineral, as is the case with chert, which is made up of silica. Rocks like chert may be referred to as monomineralic. Another example is anorthosite, which is often made up entirely of plagioclase.

Photo: Danny Christopher

Sedimentary Chemical

Gypsum

Sedimentary – Chemical – Gypsum Rock

Field Features

Look for gypsum rock in areas that have sandstone, mudstone, and siltstone. In a dry area, gypsum rock can be quite resistant to **erosion** because of the tightly interlocked minerals it contains, which form the cap rock on hills.

Textures

Gypsum rock may display strong layering. What was originally horizontal, when the rock was first formed, is often found in a contorted pattern. **Fossils** are rare.

Physical Description

Gypsum rock is white, pink, red, green, or brown. Minerals can be fine- to coarse-grained, and are usually **granular** or **fibrous**. A freshly broken piece will sparkle in the sun.

Photo: Danny Christopher

Mineral Constituents

The mineral gypsum is the main component of this eponymous rock. It is also associated with anhydrite, halite, calcite, dolomite, clay minerals, and hematite.

Environment

Gypsum is formed due to the addition of water to the mineral anhydrite. Anhydrite is originally an evaporite **deposit**. In a lake, lagoon, or shallow sea, if all the water dries up, anhydrite **crystals** can be left on the bottom. Eventually these crystals are covered by other **sediments**, pressed, and turned into a solid rock.

On Ellesmere Island, near the Eureka weather station, geologists have found many **diapirs**, which are **domes** of evaporite rock. These domes consist mostly of anhydrite and have a base of rock salt. The top surface is a gypsum rock. As well as Ellesmere, these domes can also be found on Axel Heiberg Island.

Traditional & Modern Uses

Gypsum is used as a binding and setting material for stucco and plaster. It is added to cement and is also used for lightweight indoor building materials, such as wallboard. Some gypsum is used in iron smelting, to make **soil** conditioner, and fertilizer. It is also a filler in paper products and rubber.

Did You Know?

A very compact form of gypsum rock is called alabaster. It is used for polished slabs and other decorative arts, like carvings.

Sedimentary Chemical

Iron Formation

Sedimentary – Chemical – Iron Formation

Field Features

This rock type is normally found with limestone, chert, and sandstone. Dramatic layering accentuated by colour changes is often a good indicator of iron formation. Rusty areas may also be associated with **outcrops** of iron formation, due to the high iron content of the entire rock.

Textures

Layering is very common in iron formation. Many exposures will also display folding of these layers.

Physical Description

Iron formation can be brown, red, green, or yellow. Minerals can be fine-, medium-, or coarse-grained. Sometimes round **nodules** can be seen in the rock. **Fossils** may also be visible.

Mineral Constituents

If analyzed, the chemical contents of an iron formation will be found to contain more than 15% iron. The common iron-bearing minerals that it may contain are: siderite, hematite, magnetite, pyrite, and limonite. Some detrital grains (gravel, sand, silt, or any other material produced by **erosion**) may be present. Calcite and dolomite are the common cementing agents in this rock.

Photo: Royal Ontario Museum

172

Environment

The iron-bearing minerals **crystallize** out of sea water and settle to the ocean floor, forming layers that can be thin or thick. Some layers may be less iron-rich, containing different minerals, especially very fine-grained quartz. Iron formation can form over a large area.

Bog iron ore is a rock that is formed from **sediment deposition** in lakes, lagoons, and sea water. There has to be restricted movement of bacteria in the environment for the formation of bog iron. This rock displays fine balls of clay or limonite that have rolled around on the sea, lake, or lagoon bottoms. These fine balls eventually become compacted and hardened into a porous rock.

An extensive 140-kilometre-long iron formation, called the Bravo Lake iron formation, occurs in the central part of Baffin Island, at the Qimmiq exploration project. This formation hosts several gold **occurrences** and zones. Parts of this iron formation are strongly **regionally metamorphosed**, and display strong folding. The gold is found in parts of the iron formation, which is very rich in quartz but was added to the rock as an alteration, after it had already solidified. The gold is also found in quartz **veins** that cut across the iron formation.

Traditional & Modern Uses

Very large **deposits** of iron occur in these formations. Iron is used extensively in industry. It is used to make steel and a variety of chemicals.

Many iron formations are also host to gold **mineralization**. Where enough gold occurs in a localized area, it may be possible to mine it.

Did You Know?

Some geologists think that organisms were critical to the creation of iron formation. This is a interesting theory, because most iron formations were formed during the Precambrian time of the Earth's development, over 600 million years ago. Not a lot is known about the kinds of single-celled organisms that formerly existed, nor how they contributed to creating these rocks.

Sedimentary Chemical

Limestone

Sedimentary – Biogenic or Chemical – Limestone

Field Features

Outcrops of limestone can be very thick and extensive. Look for it where other **sedimentary** rocks are present. Layers may be evident. On large outcrops, part of an original coral reef structure may be found. Limestone weathers easily and so the surface is usually crumbly, pitted, and pockmarked.

Textures

Limestone is formed in a variety of ways and is variable in appearance. It can range from being very fine-grained and porcelaneous, to coarse-grained and sugary. **Fossils** may make up a small or large part of the rock and can make the rock look like a pile of broken fossils. The type of fossil and its quantity alters the look of the rock.

Physical Description

Limestone is usually white, cream, yellow, or grey. The main constituent is calcite and the rock will fizz when diluted hydrochloric acid is poured onto it. The rock can be scratched by a knife.

Mineral Constituents

The main mineral in all limestone is calcite. Sometimes small quantities of dolomite, quartz, feldspar (either plagioclase or orthoclase), or clay minerals may be present. The fossil shells are also mostly made of calcite.

Environment

Some limestone is formed by chemical methods and some by organic methods. Chemically deposited limestone is generally coarse- to medium-grained. Sometimes little grains of calcite will roll around on the sea bottom in a shallow water environment. The little granules will get coated with more calcite and grow into small spheres. The resulting rock, an oolitic limestone, is made of these little balls.

Photo: Danny Christopher

Organic limestone usually contains an abundance of fossil fragments, all cemented by calcite. The calcite is typically fine-grained. The fossils present are generally those of organisms that lived in the warm and shallow seas: crinoids, corals, mollusks, and bryozoans. This rock's appearance is very lumpy.

Just south of Baffin Island, in the centre of Ungava Bay, lies Akpatok Island, which is made entirely of limestone. The flat plateau in the centre is surrounded by steep cliffs, 150 to 250 metres high, which rise out of the sea. Colonies of murres live on these rugged cliffs.

Traditional & Modern Uses

Limestone is widely available and has been used for building stone and decorative tiles for a long time. For example, the pyramids in Egypt are built of limestone with fossils in it. Tough limestones are used for road building.

Cement is made of limestone, as is mortar. In the steel-making industry, limestone is used as a flux, an ingredient that allows other chemical reactions to occur more easily. It is also used in the manufacture of sugar, glass, and paints.

Did You Know?

Beyond the many uses of limestone, this rock may also be host to other forms of valuable **mineralization** such as lead, zinc, fluorite, sulphur, and **oil deposits**.

Sedimentary Chemical

Rock Salt

Sedimentary – Chemical – Rock Salt

Field Features

Usually, rock salt is found close to shale, dolostone, and red sandstones. Rock salt is easily distorted and may be found in unusual forms.

Textures

Rock salt occurs in thick, featureless beds. Sometimes thin layers of shale may occur between the beds of rock salt.

Physical Description

Usually colourless or white, rock salt may be red, orange, yellow, or even purple. **Crystals** are coarse-grained and **massive**. Overall the rock will look glassy or sugary.

Mineral Constituents

Halite is the main mineral in rock salt. Halite is pure salt and therefore has a salty taste. Mixed with the halite, there can be a little calcite, dolomite, clay, or iron minerals.

Environment

Rock salt is formed when all the water in a lagoon, sea, or lake dries up and leaves behind salt **deposits**. The little bit of salt present in the water becomes very concentrated as the water gradually evaporates. This rock is considered an evaporite rock. **Evaporites** commonly form where there are deserts.

After the salt beds have formed and are buried under more **sediments**, the salt may be pushed up, like toothpaste, rising up through cracks in the overlying rocks. The resulting body is called a salt **plug** or **dome**. Sometimes **petroleum** deposits are found nearby, pooling inside of the adjacent deformed rocks.

On Axel Heiberg Island, there are springs that formed as a result of subsurface salt aquifers. An aquifer is a layer of permeable rock with many spaces and openings where large amounts of water can be stored. Water enters and leaves this salt aquifer by way of the salt **domes**, which reach the surface. On Axel Heiberg Island, the water flows down into the salt dome through tiny pores from a large lake, Phantom Lake. After it flows through the salt to a point deep underground, the current seeps back up to the surface, which creates the springs. Even though the air temperature averages 17°C, the springs flow year-round.

Traditional & Modern Uses

Salt is an important ingredient for the chemical industry and is used to produce caustic soda, chlorine, sodium, and hydrochloric acid. The industries that benefit from these chemicals include: glass, paper, textiles, leather, soap, meat and fish packaging, dairy products, and table salt.

Companies exploring for **oil deposits** will frequently search for salt **plugs**, since salt plugs are often next to oil deposits.

Did You Know?

The mining of rock salt has existed for over 3,000 years. In modern times, miners concentrate on working only the purest beds. In some hot parts of the world, shallow sea water ponds can be closed off from the rest of the sea. The ponds naturally dry up quickly, leaving behind salt so that it can be mined.

Photo: Danny Christopher

Sedimentary Chemical

Arkose

Sedimentary – Detrital – Arkose

Field Features

Arkose is normally found close to a body of granite or granite gneiss. It can also be found near conglomerate, another **sedimentary** rock.

Textures

Sometimes layers will be seen in arkose. The tops of the layers may show evidence of the direction of the current that laid down the grains. Ripple marks are another example of this phenomena. **Fossils** are rare.

Physical Description

Arkose is red, pink, or grey. Minerals are angular and generally medium-grained, nearly coarse-grained.

Mineral Constituents

At least a quarter of the rock is made of feldspar (either plagioclase or orthoclase). Most of the remainder is quartz with small quantities of biotite or muscovite. Calcite or iron rust is usually what cements the hard grains together.

Environment

Arkose is formed from the **erosion** products of granite or granite gneiss. The broken mineral pieces are carried a short distance by water and are deposited on a river bottom, along a lake shore, or on a marine coastline. These angular feldspar and quartz fragments then press together and get cemented in place with calcite.

South of Baker Lake, there is a basin full of sedimentary rocks called the Baker Lake group. The very base of this stack of rocks is an extensive arkose **unit**. In places, it hosts uranium **mineralization**.

Arkose is used locally for building stone.

Cementation of **sediment** particles happens when elements like silica or calcium are available in a fluid that moves around the particles. Like a glue, this fluid will dry and hold together the grains in the vicinity. Dolomite, siderite, and iron oxide are other common cementing materials.

Photo: Danny Christopher

Sedimentary Detrital

Breccia

Sedimentary – Detrital – Breccia

Field Features

One can expect to find breccia near conglomerate, arkose, and sandstone.

Textures

A defining feature of breccia is the angular rock fragments, which maintain sharp edges and corners. This rock is not usually layered or organized in any way. **Fossils** are rare in breccia.

Physical Description

The colour of breccia is variable and depends on the pieces of rock it contains. The rock chunks range from less than a centimetre to over a metre in size. In between the chunks, there is a fine- to medium-grained **matrix**.

Photo: Danny Christopher

Mineral Constituents

Any kind of rock pieces can make up breccia. The matrix is made of sand or silt and is cemented by quartz or calcite. Cementation happens mostly at a microscopic scale when there are very thin films of melted quartz or calcite. With the pressure on the **sediments**, there is close contact between all the pieces and, once the quartz or calcite solidifies again, the breccia is set.

Environment

A sedimentary breccia forms at the base of a cliff or very steep hill. The talus (pile of rock debris at the foot of a cliff) eventually hardens to form a new rock. Thus landslides are important in the formation of breccia. The corners of the **blocks** are sharp because the time involved in the movement of the blocks is very short and so there is no time for jostling, rubbing, and rounding off of corners.

Breccia occurs in the Bermuda sulphide showing, which is found on the northwest tip of Devon Island. In a talus slope, there are blocks of **massive** sphalerite with minor amounts of marcasite (related to pyrite) and galena. Nearby, there are also some fault breccias in which the dolostone has been broken up in a fault zone (a fault, instead of being a single, clean fracture, may be a zone consisting of many interlacing fractures), and then recemented by calcite **veins**.

Traditional & Modern Uses

Some types of breccia can be used for polished indoor stones.

Did You Know?

The term breccia is not only a rock name, but it is also used to describe what can happen to rocks that occur along a fault zone. A fault in the **crust** is a large crack, along which there is movement of the ground. The rocks, along the fracture, break and form angular blocks. This is a called a fault breccia. In a **volcanic** setting, if hardened **lava** is broken up by a new pulse of **magma**, this is also called a breccia. In all cases, breccia is the name used when the resulting rock pieces are angular, with sharp corners.

Sedimentary Detrital

Conglomerate

Sedimentary – Detrital – Conglomerate

Field Features

Conglomerate is usually found with sandstone and arkose. Conglomerate originally occurs in a river, or along the shoreline of a lake or sea. If the conglomerate is very tough and well-cemented, it will form cliffs and large, high **outcrops**. If the cement between the **clasts** (broken pieces of older rock that are cemented into a new rock) is weak, then the conglomerate will crumble into piles of loose pebbles and boulders.

Photo: Danny Christopher

Textures

Conglomerate usually displays a **massive** texture and is not layered. It is rare to find conglomerate with cobbles all oriented in one direction, stacked like discs or ovals. **Fossils** are also very rare.

Physical Description

The colour of conglomerate is highly dependent on what the pebbles and cobbles are. Conglomerate is a very distinctive rock with pebbles, cobbles, and boulders held together by a fine- or medium-grained **matrix**.

Mineral Constituents

The clasts in conglomerate are made of quartz, feldspars (either plagioclase or orthoclase), chert or tough rocks like quartzite, granite, amphibolite, gneiss, limestone, and dolostone.

Conglomerate may have all of its clasts of one rock type. Conversely, conglomerate can contain a large variety of different rock types in the clasts.

182

Environment

A rapid river is necessary to move such large rocks. The cobbles are normally rounded, with edges and corners that have been smoothed by tumbling through the forceful water system. In between the waterworn **clasts**, there is some clay and other fine minerals (quartz and feldspar) that act as a cement to hold the rock rigidly together. Along a shoreline, a vigorous event like a major storm is required to move, round off, and form accumulations of cobbles. Once **cementation** occurs, conglomerate is formed.

A variety of conglomerates have been mapped by geologists on the West Meliadine project, near Rankin Inlet. One variety consists entirely of quartz pebbles set in a matrix of biotite and chlorite. The other variety describes a range of rock types that occur in another conglomerate, which include quartz pebbles, rhyolite, and granite, all set in a cement of quartz and feldspar (either plagioclase or orthoclase).

Traditional & Modern Uses

Where the cementing material is tough and uniform throughout the rock, a conglomerate can be cut and polished for use as a building stone. Where the rock is not very well cemented, it can be used as a source of gravel.

Did You Know?

Another name for conglomerate is puddingstone. This name originated in England and France, where puddings are made with big chunks of fruit.

Photo: Royal Ontario Museum

Sedimentary Detrital

Greywacke

Sedimentary – Detrital – Greywacke

Field Features

Greywacke is a common rock and resembles a dirty sandstone. It occurs with siltstone and shale.

Textures

Greywacke commonly forms graded beds—this formation is its most distinctive feature. A bed is a layer of **sediment** that originally laid down flat. The graded beds have bottom layers with coarser sandstone grains. As the grains accumulated on the bed, they became finer and finer, so the resulting rock in the upper part is siltstone or shale. Greywacke can also be entirely **massive**, with no particular form or structure, and have no visible bedding. Slump structures, which are swirly disrupted bits of the beds that have slipped down an unstable slope may also be found. **Fossils** are rare.

Physical Description

As the name suggests, greywacke is typically grey. It may also be black and display a greenish tint. The grains that make up this **sedimentary** rock are small, sharp, and angular, set in a very fine **matrix**.

Mineral Constituents

In a coarser sandstone base, bits of quartz, feldspar (either plagioclase or orthoclase), and rock fragments can also be found. The matrix in between the grains is too fine to identify with the naked eye. The green colour, where observed, is due to chlorite.

Environment

Greywacke forms in a marine basin, often below the slope of the continental **shelf**. Strong currents of water, full of loose sediment, avalanche down the slopes to the seabed and **deposit** their load of **clasts** (broken pieces of older rock that become cemented into a new rock) in the deep water. Because this movement and **deposition** happens rapidly, the sediment is not well sorted. The short time allows only for a little bit of size sorting to occur (graded beds).

At the Meadowbank project, 70 kilometres northwest of Baker Lake, greywacke occurs near Tern Lake and south of Third Portage Lake. Here it is mixed with siltstone and shale. Chlorite is a component of the matrix and it gives the rock a greenish cast. Geologists have theorized that these greywackes were formed by the **erosion** of nearby **volcanic** rocks.

Traditional & Modern Uses

Greywacke is a very tough rock and can be used as a crushed stone for road building. It is sometimes used locally for construction.

Did You Know?

The graded beds in greywacke indicate that the rocks are not very old, relatively speaking. The finer the clasts in the bed, the higher and younger the bed's level. Thus the original upward direction at the time of **deposition** can be determined. This information helps geologists determine the original environment. Where the rocks are very highly deformed and no longer have their original attitude, this **younging** information is valuable indeed.

Photo: Danny Christopher

Sandstone

Sedimentary – Detrital – Sandstone

Field Features

Sandstones are usually found with other **sedimentary** rocks. This rock type can accumulate and form great thicknesses. Sandstone is a tough rock and tends to resist **erosion**, instead forming long ridges.

Textures

Layers are normally visible in the rock as a result of the way the grains were originally deposited. There may be impressions in the sandstone that are preserved ripple marks or other features that resulted from a current in the river. **Concretions** are common in sandstone and resemble balls. Concretions form when some extra cement pools in one sedimentary area during rock formation. **Fossils**, such as the footprint of a dinosaur, may be found in sandstone.

Photo: Danny Christopher

Physical Description

Sandstone looks just like the compacted sand that you might find on a beach. The colour of sandstone is variable. The common colours are red, brown, green, yellow, grey, and white. Individual grains are small and are all about the same size. Sandstone usually has a gritty feel.

Mineral Constituents

In sandstone, the most common mineral is quartz. Feldspar (either plagioclase or orthoclase) and mica (biotite or muscovite) are often present in smaller quantities.

Environment

Sand particles can be carried by flowing water and eventually collect in the bottoms of lakes, rivers, or seas. Later, the grains become cemented together with either more quartz, calcite, or hematite. Sand can also collect in sand dunes and, in this case, it is the wind, and not water, that carries the particles of quartz. If enough new **sediment** is deposited on top of the sand dune, then it can be compressed and cemented into a sandstone.

A large region of sandstone occurs west of Baker Lake along the Thelon and Kazan Rivers. This rock was formed about one billion years ago. Today, many exploration companies are examining this sandstone carefully because it contains important **deposits** of uranium.

Traditional & Modern Uses

In medieval times, sandstone was used extensively for building cathedrals, castles, and other important buildings.

Presently, **oil** deposits found in the pore spaces of sandstone are being open-pit mined in Alberta. These are called tar sands or oil sands. Deep in the Earth's **crust**, sandstones often act as reservoirs for oil deposits. Wells can be sunk into these reservoirs to extract the oil.

Some sandstone is used by artisans in their grinding and lapping wheels. Crushed sandstone is used in a variety of ways. For example, sandstone is often used in gardening and landscaping.

Did You Know?

Where sandstone has been cemented by calcite and the rock is exposed at the Earth's surface or used in buildings, it decays due to acid rain. Acid is capable of dissolving calcite and, over many years, tombstones and building stones crumble because of acid rain. Luckily, the amount of acid rain in our atmosphere is decreasing, so this is less of a problem than in the past.

Sedimentary Detrital

Shale or Mudstone

Sedimentary – Detrital – Shale or Mudstone

Field Features

Shale is generally found in **outcrops** with other **sedimentary** detrital rocks like sandstone and conglomerate. Look for highly layered exposures. Shales and mudstones are generally softer than other sedimentary rocks and so, over the ages, will have eroded more than the surrounding rocks, exposing receded portions of cliffs made of shale.

Textures

A relatively **massive** compacted rock of this type is called a mudstone. If the rock becomes soft and gooey when wet, it is clay. The rock is called shale once it has been pressed even more and can be split easily into sheets.

Some of the finer textures found include **fossils** and **concretions**, as well as rain prints and sun cracks. The latter form when the muddy bottom of a lake or lagoon is no longer covered by water and the hot sun starts to dry and crack the mud. These connected cracks may then be preserved forever in the hardening rock.

Physical Description

Shale can be a wide variety of colours such as dark green, blue, grey, brown, red, black, or white. The individual grains in this rock are so tiny that they cannot be seen with the naked eye. Shale is smooth to the touch.

Mineral Constituents

The grains in this rock are so tiny that they cannot be identified by the human eye, or occasionally, by microscope. Research has shown that shale usually contains clay minerals, quartz, feldspar (either plagioclase or orthoclase), and mica. There may also be significant amounts of hematite, pyrite, and gypsum. Significant amounts of **oil** may be present in the shale, in which case the rock will smell oily.

Environment

Clay is deposited in water that has little or no current (called quiet water) in lake and ocean bottoms. As further **sediments** settle above this clay, water gets squeezed out, and the clay dries and hardens to form mudstone. With time and pressure, the rock is squeezed more and eventually becomes shale.

Around the Bermuda showing on Devon Island, a large sequence of limestone is capped by very fine-grained shale, which transitions into coarser-grained siltstone and even sandstone.

Traditional & Modern Uses

Shale is used in the manufacture of bricks, pottery, and other ceramic products. **Oil** shales may contain vast quantities of oil, and new technology allows the **petroleum** industry to exploit this resource.

Did You Know?

From the fossils that may be found in shale to the interesting textures like rain prints, the ancient environment in which the rock was formed can be revealed from simply studying shale.

Photo: Danny Christopher

Sedimentary Detrital

Siltstone

Sedimentary – Detrital – Siltstone

Field Features

Siltstone usually occurs close to other detrital (gravel, sand, silt, or any other material produced by **erosion**) **sedimentary** rocks, like sandstone and shale.

Textures

Siltstone is an evenly textured rock, and is quite compact. Occasionally, siltstone is earthy, which means it looks and feels like packed earth. It may be **massive**, with no obvious form or structure, or it may show fine bands. Sometimes ripple marks and other indications reveal that this rock was formed in water with a current. **Fossils** are quite common in siltstone. Round **concretions** may also be observed.

Physical Description

Siltstone can be black, grey, brown, buff, or yellow. Grains are tiny but may just be seen with the naked eye.

Mineral Constituents

The minerals are too fine to be identified in this rock, but from microscopic study geologists know that siltstone is made up mostly of quartz and feldspar (either plagioclase or orthoclase). If there is a subtle sheen on the surface, it is from very tiny grains of muscovite or biotite.

Environment

Siltstone is a collection of loose grains of silt that have been so compacted that a hard rock forms. It originates from the bottom of a lake, the sea, or from the gravels that a glacier leaves behind once it melts.

Photo: Danny Christopher

On Devon Island there is an abundance of siltstone and shale. Both rock types were formed there about 500 million years ago and the siltstone sits on top of gneiss.

Traditional & Modern Uses

Although it is an interesting rock to study, primarily because of the fossils it contains, siltstone is not economically important.

Did You Know?

A study of the types of fossils contained in the rock reveals much about the environment at the time of rock formation.

Sedimentary Detrital

Coal

Sedimentary – Organic – Coal

Field Features

Coal is generally found in areas where other continental **sediments** are found. These sediments form on top of continental **crust** rather than over oceanic crust. Coal stands out quite dramatically against the other sediments due to its black colour.

Textures

Coal has an even texture and looks like it has been melted together. Often plant remains can be seen in this rock.

Physical Description

Though generally black in colour, coal may also be brown or dark steely grey. Sometimes there are shiny and dull layers alternating throughout the coal. Coal is dirty to handle, hard, and **brittle**. There may be glassy spots. Some coal is blocky (large angular chunks of rock), while some is splintery (looks like broken wood).

Mineral Constituents

Coal is composed mostly of carbon, hydrogen, and oxygen. Some sulphur and nitrogen may be present. Small amounts of pyrite and quartz may also be found in coal.

Environment

Extensive beds of coal were formed in prehistoric lagoons, swamps, or lakes, mostly from the Paleozoic age of the Earth's history. Peat and other plant materials were covered by a thin layer of sediment and, as the pressure on the peat increased, water was driven out of the layer. In situations where the temperature increased in the peaty beds, the **volatiles** or **gases** present were also driven off. As new sediments were deposited on top of the compressed peat, the initial peat layer was buried deeper and deeper in the Earth's crust. This caused the pressure and temperature in this lower layer to rise. The remaining material was pressed into coal. If coal is metamorphosed extensively, it turns into graphite.

In Nunavut, coal forms extensive beds on the islands of the Sverdrup Basin, which includes Axel Heiberg, Ellef Ringnes, Amund Ringnes, Bylot, and Ellesmere.

Traditional & Modern Uses

In Pond Inlet, the local population mined coal in the springtime and used it to heat homes and cook. An old federal regulation allows for coal mining in Nunavut for personal use only and permission is sought from the Royal Canadian Mountain Police (RCMP) to do this.

Coal is the most abundant fossil fuel on the planet and is widely used to heat homes, cook food, and power energy plants that produce electricity. Coal is also used in the iron and steel-making industries, the synthetic rubber industry, and the dye industry.

Did You Know?

A particularly hard form of coal that takes a good polish is called jet. It is used as a semi-precious **gemstone** for ornaments and jewellery.

Photo: Danny Christopher

Sedimentary Organic

Calc-Silicate

Metamorphic – Contact – Calc-Silicate

Field Features

Calc-silicate is usually found within a large area of **sedimentary** rocks. In the vicinity, there will be an **igneous intrusion**, which provided the heat source for the **contact metamorphism**.

Textures

Sometimes it is possible to see the original sedimentary bedding preserved in this **metamorphic** rock. Calc-silicate may be **massive**, though without obvious layering.

Physical Description

Grey, pink, red, yellow-brown, or light green are the most common colours. It is similar in appearance to marble, but is rarely pure white. Minerals are medium- to coarse-grained. Some minerals may be much larger than others.

Mineral Constituents

Calcite is the main mineral in calc-silicate. There may also be a small amount of olivine, serpentine, tremolite, epidote, plagioclase, pyroxene, or garnet in this rock, normally in layers or patches.

Environment

Calc-silicate is formed in the same way as marble, except that calc-silicate is formed from an impure limestone, while marble is formed from pure. For calc-silicate, the original rock has to contain some sandy or muddy materials. Then, when the metamorphism occurs, some of the elements from these impurities combine to form the accessory minerals.

Calc-silicate occurs at the southern end of Baffin Island. There is also calc-silicate at Crook's Inlet, which contains purple pyroxene and phlogopite.

Most famous are the calc-silicate **lenses**, which host the sapphire **mineralization** near Kimmirut. Small **pods** of this rock contain a remarkable variety of minerals. A few of the main minerals found in the calc-silicate include the following: phlogopite, purple and green pyroxene, scapolite, plagioclase, calcite, graphite, and, of course, blue sapphire. The scapolite is a rare, pale yellow mineral with a unique property: it **fluoresces** an ultraviolet light when it lights up. Because scapolite is only found near the sapphire **occurrences**, geologists and prospectors can shine ultraviolet light on the **outcrops**, in order to find more exposures with scapolite and sapphire.

Traditional & Modern Uses

Some nicely coloured varieties are used for building stone, but are incorrectly called marble.

Did You Know?

Skarn is a similar rock, but skarn usually contains some metallic or sulphide minerals, such as pyrite and chalcopyrite. Geologists define a rock as mineralized when it contains some minerals of potential economic interest, therefore skarn is a mineralized calc-silicate.

Photo: Danny Christopher

Metamorphic Contact

195

Hornfels

Metamorphic – Contact – Hornfels

Field Features

The original rock textures near an **igneous intrusion** become obliterated due to the heat. If the **unit** is followed away from the intrusion and back to its original form, the change in rock textures can be observed. The hornfels rock may have a baked look very near the intrusion. The outer surface may be grey to white, with a bleached appearance.

Textures

Generally, this is a spotted rock, with large to very large mineral grains distributed throughout fine- to medium-grained **massive crystals**. The large crystals are randomly oriented. The fine minerals form a mosaic pattern, but they are usually too fine to be identified with the naked eye.

Physical Description

Hornfels is normally tough and splintery (like broken wood), because the crystals have reformed into a tight, interlocking mass. The rock is usually dark and typically brown, green, purple, black, or grey.

Mineral Constituents

The minerals observed will depend on what the rock was prior to **metamorphism**. Often the finer minerals within hornfels include quartz, mica, and pyroxene. The large minerals might be cordierite, pyroxene, garnet, or chiastolite (a variety of andalusite), along with other minerals.

Environment

Hornfels is formed in the contact **aureole** around a large igneous intrusion. The intrusion is often granite. The immense heat coming from the new intrusion recrystallizes many minerals in the contact **aureole zone**. Any rock can be converted to hornfels: igneous, **sedimentary**, and even **metamorphic rocks**. Conversion depends on what rock was in the area where the granite intruded. In general, the most metamorphosed rock is pressed up against the granite. Away from the intrusion, the **metamorphism** diminishes until the rock appears unchanged. The appearance of the original unchanged rocks marks the edge of the contact aureole.

Near Izok Lake, in the southwest Kitikmeot region, there are large **deposits** of copper and zinc. The **volcanic** and sedimentary rocks have been criss-crossed by granitic pegmatite and diabase **dikes**. Most rocks in this region turned into pyroxene hornfels.

Traditional & Modern Uses

Hornfels has been quarried for use as a crushed rock, especially in quarries where diabase is already being mined.

Did You Know?

Hornfels looks a lot like basalt, but it is harder. It also breaks into sharp chips, so be sure to wear safety glasses when hammering on this rock.

Photo: Danny Christopher

Metamorphic Contact

197

Skarn

Metamorphic – Contact – Skarn

Field Features

Exposures of skarn are generally small and are found adjacent to **igneous** rock, such as granite or syenite.

Textures

Layering or clumps of minerals may be visible. Sometimes the minerals are arranged in a radiating pattern (like the spokes in a wheel).

Physical Description

A skarn is typically brown, black, or grey. The grains can be any size. If the grains are very large and colourful then the skarn may look quite blotchy.

Mineral Constituents

Calcite is the main mineral found in skarn. Others that occur are olivine, epidote, serpentine, tremolite, pyroxene, garnet, vesuvianite, and wollastonite. Some sulphide minerals are usually present, such as pyrite, chalcopyrite, galena, and sphalerite.

Environment

When limestone is heated due to a nearby igneous **intrusion**, changes occur in the movement of some fluid and **gases** throughout the rock. In addition to simple **contact metamorphism**, there is the introduction of new elements into the rock, which results in the creation of skarn rock. The main difference between calc-silicate and skarn is that skarn contains the sulphide minerals.

In the Kimmirut area, the sapphire host rock is skarn. This particular skarn contains scapolite, which **fluoresces** yellow under an ultraviolet light. Scapolite is more widespread than sapphire, so scapolite is easier to locate, often being found in areas that may have sapphire. Scapolite is pale yellow and usually shows a few high-quality **crystal** faces.

Traditional & Modern Uses

Nicely coloured varieties of skarn are used for building stone, but they are called marble by the industry. Where there are enough sulphide minerals present, the skarn may be mined for its metal content. Some skarn contains a lot of garnet, which is mined and used for sandpaper and other abrasives.

Did You Know?

Skarn is worth locating, as many good mineral specimens can be found within it.

Photo: Shutterstone.com

Metamorphic Contact

Amphibolite

Metamorphic – Regional – Amphibolite

Field Features

Amphibolite is quite a tough rock and usually will not display any **deformation**. However, if the rocks around the amphibolite are extremely deformed, then the amphibolite might be pulled apart into large oval chunks. The mineral grains that make up the amphibolite are very tightly interlocked and resist physical changes. Amphibolite can commonly be found in areas with abundant **metamorphic** rocks.

Textures

Usually amphibolite is quite **massive**, with most minerals oriented randomly throughout the rock. Occasionally, however, all the mineral grains in this rock have their flat faces lying parallel to one another, which resembles a stack of papers. Large red grains may be seen scattered throughout the rock. Occasionally, **banding** of light- and dark-coloured minerals is present.

Physical Description

Amphibolite is green, dark green, or black. There may be **streaks** or flecks of grey, red, or white. Minerals are medium- to coarse-grained.

Mineral Constituents

As the name suggests, this rock consists mostly of amphibole. From the amphibole family, hornblende is the most common mineral found in amphibolite. Sometimes, actinolite and tremolite can be found. Other minerals that may be included are plagioclase, chlorite, biotite, epidote, pyroxene, and garnet.

Environment

Metamorphism of diabase and basalt, or less commonly impure limestone and impure dolostone, leads to the formation of amphibolite. In other words, during **mountain-building** events that crumple and crush the **crust**, the added pressure and temperature causes amphibolite to form.

Traditional & Modern Uses

Amphibolite is so tough that it makes a good crushed rock for road beds because it provides a layer of sharp rocks that do not settle easily under the asphalt. The sheetlike amphibolite can be split and used for slabs, such as patio stones.

Did You Know?

Possibly the most famous **outcrops** of amphibolite in Nunavut occur near the mouth of Frobisher Bay on Kodlunarn Island. It was here, in 1576, that Martin Frobisher landed and collected shiploads of rock, which he said contained vast amounts of gold. Scientists recently studied all the rocks on the island and found that the pits were dug on amphibolite outcrops. Amphibolite does not usually contain any significant amounts of gold and history suggests that incompetence or fraud occurred.

Photo: Danny Christophe

Metamorphic Regional

Eclogite

Metamorphic – Regional – Eclogite

Field Features

Eclogite occurs in small, restricted exposures. In particular it occurs as **lenses** and **blocks** (large angular chunks of rock that were ripped up from solidified **lava** or from rocks adjacent to **volcanic vents**) in other **igneous** and **metamorphic** rocks. Look for it in serpentinite, peridotite, and kimberlite.

Textures

Some **banding** may be visible, but usually the minerals are all jumbled in a **massive** fashion.

Physical Description

Eclogite is mottled red and green, sometimes with brownish red spots. Minerals are medium- to coarse-grained. Very large grains of garnet and pyroxene may be scattered throughout the rock.

Mineral Constituents

Key minerals in eclogite are green pyroxene (omphacite) and red garnet (pyrope). Kyanite and diamond may even be found.

Environment

Eclogite is formed in the upper **mantle** of the Earth. Eclogite originates from a rock that contains a lot of iron and magnesium, such as basalt. Basalt is formed at the Earth's surface and is transported to great depths by the action of **plate tectonics**. **Regional metamorphism** affects this rock. For eclogite to be visible and at the surface, the rock had to have been transported from these depths, either along a **fault** (a fracture in the Earth's **crust** where the rock masses on either side are offset), or by means of a moving kimberlite.

In the Jericho kimberlite (Kitikmeot region), there are abundant fragments of eclogite. The eclogite here contains a lot of red garnet, green pyroxene, and needles of rutile. There are smaller amounts of zircon, apatite, kyanite, olivine, different pyroxenes and garnets, amphibole, epidote, phlogopite, chlorite, serpentine, and ilmenite. It is estimated that this eclogite was formed at depths of 90 to 195 kilometres. Eclogite represents what the depths of Nunavut may look like.

Traditional & Modern Uses

Occasionally, gem-quality eclogite is found, where beautiful green pyroxenes and red garnets combine in a hard and dense rock. Eclogite would be used more as a crushed stone for building projects and decorative slabs if it were not such a rare rock.

Did You Know?

Eclogite is a very dense rock and will feel very heavy for its size because the **crystals** that form are very tightly packed together. This density stems from the fact that it originally formed at great depths in the earth, where the pressure and temperature are tremendous.

Photo: Danny Christopher

Gneiss

Metamorphic – Regional – Gneiss

Field Features

Gneiss is often found in the centre of an area that has been affected by **regional metamorphism**. Nearby there are often granite and pegmatite **outcrops**.

Textures

The minerals in this rock are separated into light- and dark-coloured bands. These bands can be narrow, wide, straight, or very wiggly. Sometimes the edges of the bands are very sharp, and other times they are fuzzy. Generally, the bands are not very long and it is clear where they stop abruptly.

Where large rounded feldspar minerals are scattered throughout the gneiss, these minerals tend to be eye-shaped. This distinct gneiss is called *augen gneiss*. *Augen* means eyes in German.

Photo: Royal Ontario Museum

Physical Description

Streaks and layers of grey, pink, black, and white are the most common colours. The minerals are medium- to coarse-grained. In the dark bands, the minerals are flat and all stacked to create a **foliation**. In the light bands, the minerals are round and **granular**.

Mineral Constituents

The feldspar minerals orthoclase and plagioclase, along with quartz, form the light bands. The dark bands consist of biotite or hornblende. In smaller quantities, muscovite, garnet, cordierite, and sillimanite may be found.

Environment

Gneiss is a common rock because many types of rocks, once metamorphosed, become gneiss. When a large area of the Earth's **crust** undergoes regional metamorphism, gneiss results. In an area where mountains are growing and the crust is crumpled, the added heat and pressure on the rocks cause some minerals to melt and recrystallize into a different pattern. The **occurrence** of gneiss indicates that, formerly, there were mountains in an area.

Photo: Royal Ontario Museum

Examples of gneiss are abundant in the glacially deposited cobbles and boulders that litter the ground everywhere in Nunavut. Around Iqaluit, it is easy to find gneiss in all the hills around town. If you look carefully, you will see that there is garnet and pyrite in the gneiss. The original **igneous** rock was granodiorite and, after metamorphism, much of this rock transformed into granodiorite gneiss.

Traditional & Modern Uses

Gneiss is used as building stone and as crushed rock.

Did You Know?

The word *gneiss* is pronounced "nice." It is an old German word that means "spark," and refers to the rock's sheen.

Photo: Danny Christopher

Metamorphic Regional

Granulite

Metamorphic – Regional – Granulite

Field Features

Granulite is found in areas with other **metamorphic** rocks. It is generally found in the **craton** of the largest continents.

Textures

Granulite is formed under very high pressure and therefore the rock may look like a stack of paper, especially along one edge. Sometimes bands can be observed.

Physical Description

Normally white or very light-coloured, granulite is made of minerals that are fine- to medium-grained. Often the rock is **massive**, with no discernible orientation or pattern to the **crystals**.

Photo: Shutterstone.com

Mineral Constituents

Granulite contains a lot of feldspar (either plagioclase or orthoclase), and flat plates of quartz. Other minerals commonly found are pyroxene, garnet, kyanite, and sillimanite.

One variety of granulite, called charnockite, does not display the garnet or the **platy** style quartz. The key ingredient in granulite is a pyroxene mineral called hypersthene.

Environment

Granulite results from very high levels of **metamorphism**, which occur deep in the Earth's **crust** (at least 30 kilometres down). The very high pressure and temperature of the lower crust region cause minerals in a rock to transform into other minerals.

For granulite to be observed at the Earth's surface, it must undergo much **deformation** and crustal movement.

A charnockite granulite occurs in the area around Pangnirtung. It is composed largely of two feldspars, perthite and andesine. In addition, it also contains pyroxene (hypersthene). Minor minerals are quartz, hornblende, and magnetite. Charnockite is white with blue spots.

Traditional & Modern Uses

These days granulite is used as crushed stone for building projects. It is extremely tough, and it is pressure- and weather-resistant. Some varieties are turned into polished slabs.

Did You Know?

The charnockite variety of granulite is a very uncommon rock. It was first noted for its unique properties when it was used for Job Charnock's gravestone in Calcutta, India. The stone was named for Job Charnock, who was the founder of Calcutta.

Granulite is essentially a mica-free gneiss, thus it will never contain biotite, muscovite, or phlogopite. A lack of mica is unusual, as most metamorphic rocks are full of mica.

Metamorphic *Regional*

Marble

Metamorphic – Contact and Regional – Marble

Field Features

Marble is usually found close to a large **igneous intrusion**. There may also be limestone near marble sites, since marble is created from limestone. Marble is also formed during **regional metamorphism** and is therefore usually found close to schist and quartzite. Compared to other rocks, marble is softer and more easily eroded, and therefore it will form basins or recessed areas. In these cases the surface will also be crumbly.

Photo: Danny Christopher

Textures

If the changes that the rock has undergone are weak, some of the original horizontal layering may still be visible. As the strength of metamorphism increases, those **sedimentary** textures disappear. **Fossils** may also be present.

Physical Description

Generally, marble is white or grey, but it may display **streaks** of green, red, or black. Individual grains are medium to coarse and will often look like sugar. If the marble is made up largely of calcite, then it will dissolve and bubble when weak hydrochloric acid is poured on it. Thin pieces of marble will be transparent.

Mineral Constituents

Marble is made up of calcite. It may also contain dolomite. In small quantities serpentine, olivine, tremolite, or phlogopite may be observed.

Environment

Marble is created when limestone makes contact with a very hot igneous intrusion, during the process whereby **magma** slowly solidifies. Marble is also formed from limestone during the process of regional metamorphism. When two crustal plates smash into one another, the **crust** will buckle and fold. In the tightest parts of the folds, the temperature and pressure increases, which changes the solid rocks.

Close to Kimmirut, and around the sapphire **occurrences**, there is abundant marble. The marble is white to buff-coloured and some of the original bedding is still visible. Besides the calcite, this rock also contains some phlogopite, diopside, graphite, and apatite.

Traditional & Modern Uses

Marble is used for interior and exterior architecture, tabletops, ornaments, and cladding. It takes a polish quite well, but can quickly become dull when exposed to air. Lesser grade marble is used as a crushed stone in construction, as railroad ballast, and filter beds (basins filled with materials through which liquids are filtered). A dolomite-rich marble may be mined for the extraction of magnesium.

Did You Know?

The word marble comes from the Greek language and means "shimmering block of stone."

Photo: Danny Christopher

Metamorphic Regional

Migmatite

Metamorphic – Regional – Migmatite

Field Features

Look for migmatites in areas of strong **regional metamorphism**. They can also form in the **contact zone** around a very hot **igneous intrusion**. Usually migmatites are found in **cratons**, which are some of the oldest continental **crusts** on Earth.

Textures

Migmatite is made of two different rock types with very sharp boundaries between them. Both components of the migmatite may display a gneiss texture, that is, dramatically alternating dark and light layers. Flat minerals will often be aligned in the same direction. The granite portion of this rock forms layers, **pods**, or **veins**. Swirling folds and intricate designs may be found in this rock, which is evidence of the strong **deformation** that affected it.

Physical Description

A darker-coloured rock type is mixed with a lighter-coloured granite rock, either grey, pink, or white. All the minerals are medium- to coarse-grained.

Mineral Constituents

The granite segments of a migmatite contain mostly orthoclase and quartz. The dark layers represent remnants of the original host rock and can be made up of any number of minerals.

Environment

A migmatite is a highly metamorphosed rock. Much deformation has affected the migmatite in the same way that plastic can be bent and moulded into new shapes, when enough temperature and pressure are applied.

Migmatite forms at great depths in the Earth's crust, and it is only through billions of years of **uplift** and **erosion** that these rocks make their way to the surface of the Earth where we can see them.

In the central Baffin Island region, around Lake Gillian and Pedro Lake, there are abundant migmatites. Plenty of metamorphosed **sedimentary** rocks occur in this area. In the most highly metamorphosed areas, migmatite is found with orthoclase, cordierite, sillimanite, and garnet.

Traditional & Modern Uses

Migmatite can make a very attractive polished slab and ornamental stone.

Did You Know?

Two main theories exist regarding the formation of migmatite. The first theory is that it may have been formed from the partial melting of the deep crust, with the melted bits of **magma** injected back into certain local layers in the rock. Because this process involves a liquid magma, some geologists will call this rock igneous and not **metamorphic**.

The second theory of migmatite formation involves the replacement of one element in a mineral by a second element. This replacement happens when a hot liquid moves along minute cracks and spaces, melting and replacing the second mineral as it moves. Eventually one mineral becomes replaced entirely by another mineral of different composition.

Metamorphic Regional

Phyllite

Metamorphic – Regional – Phyllite

Field Features

Phyllite is found in areas with other metamorphosed **sedimentary** rocks, such as marble and schist. Phyllite is often found in **outcrops** with jagged and irregular outlines. These outcrops show evidence of **folding**. Much irregular **erosion** will be evident as slabs of the phyllite break off.

Textures

Due to a high proportion of flat, **platy** minerals, phyllite splits easily into flat sheets. The split surfaces may reveal little corrugations (grooves or ridges) or larger folds.

Physical Description

The distinctive characteristic of phyllite is its silvery sheen. The rock is usually green or grey. Individual minerals are fine- to medium-grained. The rock may be spotted with larger garnet or plagioclase grains.

Mineral Constituents

When the phyllite is greenish, chlorite is the main mineral. In grey phyllite, muscovite is the principal mineral. Quartz is another common mineral. Biotite, feldspar (either plagioclase or orthoclase), graphite, and epidote may also occur in phyllite.

Environment

Phyllite is a result of the early stages of **regional metamorphism** of shale or mudstone. If the metamorphism continues with higher temperatures and pressures, the resulting rock is schist.

At the former Lupin gold mine in the Kitikmeot region, chlorite-rich phyllite is commonly observed above the main iron formation. Other rocks nearby are greywacke and garnet schist.

Photo: Danny Christopher

Traditional & Modern Uses

Phyllite has been used for roofing tiles, but it is sensitive to frost.

Did You Know?

The name is derived from the Greek word for leaves, *phyllos*.

Quartzite

Metamorphic – Regional – Quartzite

Field Features

This white rock is easily spotted from a distance, and generally forms high hills. The surface of the rock is often polished smooth by the grinding action of ancient glaciers that have passed over the land. Quartzite can be found in the same area as **outcrops** of schist, marble, and phyllite.

Textures

The texture of quartzite resembles a large quantity of sugar. The grains of quartz that make up this rock are very tightly interlocked, creating a very even look. Some layering in the rock and even some evidence of **sedimentary** structures, like ripples and other marks made by the current, can be observed.

Physical Description

Quartzite is made of a very hard mineral and is much harder than white marble, a rock that is similar in appearance. Look for a rock that is white, grey, brownish, or reddish. Minerals are normally small and fine-grained.

Mineral Constituents

As its name suggests, this rock is made up largely of quartz **crystals**. There may be a small amount of feldspar (either plagioclase or orthoclase) or some muscovite. Very small quantities of chlorite, magnetite, hematite, garnet, and graphite may occur in quartzite.

Photo: Danny Christopher

Environment

In areas affected by **regional metamorphism**, sandstone will convert to quartzite. As the sandstone is buried by new **sediments** laid overtop, some of the quartz grains recrystallize into a tough cement. The sand grains become so tightly welded together that if the rock is struck with a hammer the fractures will pass through a quartz grain rather than along the cemented boundaries. Fracturing is a key way to distinguish quartzite sandstone.

At Marble Island, just offshore from Rankin Inlet, the stark white rocks are immediately striking. This important cluster of islands has immense historical and spiritual significance to Nunavummiut. Early European explorers mistakenly called the rock marble based simply on the rock's white colour and the wavy lines that run through it. In actual fact, these islands consist of quartzite, which is a much harder rock than marble. **Stylolites** (squiggly lines running through a rock) occur in sandstone and quartzite, as well as in marble. They were formed while the rock was being squeezed by uneven vertical pressure. Some areas were pushed down more than others. At the same time, this squeezing caused some minerals to melt into a fluid form, which was then pressed out of the rock.

Traditional & Modern Uses

Due to its **hardness** and strength, quartzite is often used as crushed stone in road building. When there is more muscovite in the rock, it tends to split into platelike sheets and is then used for flooring and tile work. Very pure quartzite is used to manufacture glass, ceramics, and fire-resistant stones, such as those in a wood-burning stove.

Did You Know?

There is a type of quartzite from the Minas Gerais district in Brazil, that has just enough muscovite to make thin sheets of it flexible. Muscovite is flexible and elastic, which is one of its interesting physical properties. We often think of rocks as rigid and unchanging, but this is obviously not so!

Metamorphic *Regional*

Schist

Metamorphic – Regional – Schist

Field Features

Schist occurs with other rocks produced by **regional metamorphism**. Schist can gradually merge into gneiss. Often the schist will be **folded**, with the bent lines made by the edges of the mineral sheets. On its own, the schist will not form high hills or ridges.

Textures

The **platy** overall texture gives this rock the appearance of a stack of papers or leaves. Schist can be split into large sheets or slabs by using a chisel.

Physical Description

In schist, all the minerals have a platy appearance and are lined up in the same direction. Usually the minerals are coarse and can be identified with the naked eye. The colour of schist is highly variable and will depend on the main mineral constituents.

Mineral Constituents

Mica and clay minerals are predominantly expected in schist. Muscovite and biotite occur alongside quartz. Other common constituents are chlorite, kyanite, graphite, garnet, talc, and sillimanite. Some minerals, like garnet, are round and will form knots in the otherwise platy schist.

Environment

Shale, mudstone, rhyolite, basalt, and other **metamorphic** rocks convert to schist when affected by regional metamorphism.

Schist is a common rock type and is widespread in Nunavut. Around Meliadine Lake, just west of Rankin Inlet, schists have been formed from greywacke, a **sedimentary** rock. These schists are rich in muscovite and biotite. Locally, schist rocks gradually merge into gneiss.

Traditional & Modern Uses

Slabs of schist with a high quartz content can be used for building stone. Sometimes schist can be mined for the main mineral it contains. For example, graphite schist is mined for its high graphite content. Chlorite schist may be ground and carved on a lathe for use in ornamental objects.

Did You Know?

In rock names, often a mineral name will be first, as with chlorite schist, which indicates that chlorite is the predominant mineral in that rock.

Photo: Danny Christopher

Serpentinite

Metamorphic – Regional – Serpentinite

Field Features

Serpentinite is commonly **banded** and occurs with other rocks that have been tightly **folded** and deformed. Many polished surfaces are common and some will display fine ridges.

Textures

Serpentinite has a compact look, with the grains very tightly packed together. It is typically medium-grained and the minerals are easy to identify, but it can also be so fine-grained that a microscope is required to spot the grains.

Photo: Danny Christopher

Physical Description

Serpentinite is usually blotchy or irregular in colour, with patches or stripes of dark red, green, yellow, and black. Its appearance is dull to waxy, or even felted. The rock will feel greasy and somewhat smooth.

Mineral Constituents

This rock is almost entirely composed of various serpentine minerals, such as antigorite and chrysotile. Some bits of olivine may be present. In much smaller quantities, there could be some garnet, pyroxene, calcite, hornblende, mica, chlorite, talc, magnetite, or chromite.

Environment

Serpentinite forms in narrow **dikes** and **stocks** and as **lenses**. Normally the rock starts out as peridotite or pyroxenite and changes to a serpentinite with the introduction of serpentine through **regional metamorphism**.

This rock is found where mountains are being built up. Mountain creation occurs when two **continental plates** collide, moving past one another, and where the **crust** is folded up.

Traditional & Modern Uses

Serpentinite rock bodies provide the mineral asbestos, used for making heat-resistant products. **Nuggets** of platinum are sometimes associated with layers of serpentinite. It can also host iron **ore deposits**, chromite, copper, or nickel deposits. For this reason, serpentinite has been used for making pots. As a facing stone for buildings or ornamental stone, it is beautiful but sometimes does not endure in harsh weather.

Inuit have long used this rock for carving beautiful sculptures and for making the qulliq, a traditional oil lamp. The Mary River–Nuluujaak Mountain area deposit, found in July 1981, supplies Pond Inlet, Clyde River, Igloolik, and Hall Beach with stone for sculpting.

Did You Know?

The name for this rock arose from its blotchy patterns, resembling scales on snakes or serpents.

Metamorphic Regional

Slate

Metamorphic – Regional – Slate

Field Features

When slate is encountered in the field, it is often **folded** and if it contains **fossils**, they are often distorted as well. The edges of the **outcrop** can be jagged and flaky. Other **metamorphic** rocks will be found nearby.

Textures

This rock is always dense and fine-grained and, generally, individual grains cannot be detected. A characteristic texture is that of its **cleavage**. This rock splits easily into thin, flat sheets.

Physical Description

While slate is often black, it can also be blue, purple, green, buff, and brown. Phyllite is a similar rock type, but generally displays a silvery sheen across the cleavage surfaces.

Mineral Constituents

While the minerals are generally too fine to be identified, occasionally pyrite can be observed in small, brassy cubes. Quartz and muscovite are generally present. Grey and black slates contain bitumen (**petroleum**) or graphite. Brown slates contain limonite (an iron rust). A red slate gets its colour from hematite, whereas a green slate arises from the presence of chlorite.

Environment

Slate is formed by the low-grade **regional metamorphism** of shale. During the collision of crustal plates, mountain ranges are created by crumpling. The intense pressure and heat that is generated changes the rock from what was originally shale or mudstone (or sometimes ash tuff) to slate.

Spotted slates, with a coarser-grained mineral (andalusite or cordierite are common), indicates the rock was changed by the high heat, which came from contact with an **igneous intrusion**. It is almost as if the slate has been burned.

East of High Lake, in the Kitikmeot region, a slate **unit** can be found along the Kennarctic River. It is black and thinly bedded. This rock is highly deformed. The slate is found alongside a siltstone.

Photo: Danny Christopher

Traditional & Modern Uses

Slate was used to make blackboards for classrooms and meeting rooms. It is now used for roofing, flooring, wall tiles, insulating slabs, and electrical switchplates.

Did You Know?

Sometimes the original bedding planes in shale are preserved in the metamorphosed slate. As the rock is deformed and folded, the cleavage angle is generally some degrees off from the bedding plane angle. The result can be pencil slate, in which rods of slate that resemble pencils may break off the outcrop.

Meteorite

Extraterrestrial – Meteorite

Field Features

Meteorites in Antarctica, which in some ways has a similar environment to the Arctic, are found in gravel **deposits** where the ice melted, retreated, and deposited its load of rock. The meteorites that are trapped in Antarctic ice are very well preserved, and some have been held in the ice for over a million years.

Textures

If an iron meteorite is cut open, then etched with acid, a complex intergrowth of the metallic minerals is revealed. Iron meteorites are often irregular in shape, with many bumps. Stony meteorites can be worn down by the high-speed travel through the atmosphere, forming cone and **dome** shapes.

Physical Description

There are two main types of meteorites: stony and iron. A third, but less common, variety exhibits properties of both. First, look for the presence of chondrules, which are little round bodies throughout a stony meteorite. Second, meteorites always have a fusion **crust**, a very thin black coating that is usually only found on one side of the stone. Lastly, look for a nickel-iron **alloy** in iron meteorites, which may make up the entire rock, or at least occur as shiny scattered grains and patches.

Mineral Constituents

Iron meteorites are mostly made of nickel and iron metals. They are mixed together in a complex intergrowth that occurred when the rock was formed.

Stony meteorites are by far the most common. They contain the spheres called chondrules. The main minerals observed are from the silicate family and include pyroxene, olivine, and plagioclase, along

Photo: Royal Ontario Museum

with some nickel and iron minerals.

Environment

Meteorites originate in the Asteroid Belt primarily, although 20 or so meteorites have been from the moon. When an object hits the moon with enough force to create a crater, rock material is thrown up into space. Eventually this material arrives on Earth. Similarly, this is how some meteorites arrive here from Mars.

When the meteorite strikes the Earth, it may create a crater if it is large. The **bedrock** shatters and instantly melts, with very rare and unusual minerals forming from this melted liquid.

Photo: Royal Ontario Museum

Traditional & Modern Uses

Scientists study meteorites carefully because they indicate the composition and early history of the solar system. Also, some scientists believe that meteorites resemble the centre of our planet.

Did You Know?

Meteorites range in size from tiny as a pebble to larger than a house. When they zoom through the Earth's atmosphere, they glow red and have a long tail. This is what we call a shooting star. Very large meteorites hit the Earth at speeds between 20 to 70 kilometres per second! At such high speed, often the meteorite vaporizes, or disintegrates into tiny pieces when it hits the ground.

Extraterrestrial

Glossary

acicular: Long and needlelike.

acicular

adamantine: Brilliantly shiny, like a diamond.

aeolian: Produced by the wind.

agglomerate: (Of blocks and fragments) Formed through the explosive activity of a volcano.

aggregate: A collection or grouping of crystals.

alteration product: When a mineral changes to something else due to the presence of a hot fluid, or the action of weathering.

anhydrous: Completely without water.

alloy: A substance that is a mixture of two or more metals.

alluvial fan: Deposit of clay, silt, sand, and gravel left by a flowing river.

alluvial fan

ash: Uncemented fragments of rock erupted by a volcano that are less than 4 millimetres in diameter.

asterism: A six-rayed, starlike effect observed in a mineral, resulting from light shining off minute inclusions inside the mineral that are arranged along regular atomic structure lines.

atom: The basic unit of a chemical element.

atomic structure: The form in which atoms combine into molecules.

aureole zone: Zone around an igneous intrusion where contact metamorphism of the country rocks has taken place.

axis/axes (pl.): A line about which the crystal can be rotated and still show symmetry.

banding: Alternating or varying mineralogy, colours, or textures.

banding

batholith: A very large igneous intrusion that can go deep in the Earth's crust.

bedrock: The crustal rock found at the Earth's surface. It can be totally exposed, or covered with soil or other unconsolidated material, like glacial till.

biogenic: Produced or brought about by living organisms.

block: Large, angular chunks of rock that were ripped up from solidified lava or from rocks adjacent to volcanic vents.

bomb: A chunk of lava that solidifies as it flies through the air.

botryoidal: Resembling a cluster of grapes.

brittle: Easily reduced to fragments with a light blow.

cementation: Precipitation of a binding material that glues sedimentary grains together. Quartz, calcite, dolomite, siderite, and iron oxide are common cementing materials.

clast: Broken piece of older rock that becomes cemented to a new rock.

cleavage: The way a mineral breaks along well-defined planes of weakness, or the way a crystal breaks into regular fragments, resulting in smooth, flat surfaces.

cleavage plane: Surface where a mineral naturally fractures.

columnar: Columnlike.

columnar jointing: Six-sided columns that are topped with flat surfaces and erode to different heights, creating a steplike exposure.

complex: Grouping or collection of rocks.

concentric: Layers arranged in a circular fashion, like the various candy layers in a jawbreaker; circular.

conchoidal: Clam-shaped.

concretions: When minerals grow around a central point or nucleus, forming balls; where a ball of mud forms around a foreign object.

contact metamorphism: Process through which rocks are changed because of heat from a hot magma body.

contact zone: A zone surrounding an igneous intrusion in which contact metamorphism of the country rock has taken place.

contacts: The place where two different rock types touch.

continental plate: The crust that underlies a continent.

country rocks: The basic geological formations underlying a region; the pre-existing rock surrounding an igneous intrusion.

cockscomb aggregate: A grouping that looks like a fan with spear-shaped segments.

craton: Large stable block of the Earth's crust forming the nucleus of a continent.

crystal: A mineral with a regular geometric shape.

crystallize: To form or cause crystals to form.

crust: The thin outer layer of the Earth, extending down to the Mohorovicic Discontinuity; the crust under continents is granitic and 30 to 40 kilometres thick; oceanic crust is basaltic and approximately 7 to 13 kilometres thick.

crusted: A thin layer or coating that conforms to any irregularities in the underlying substrate.

deformation: Change in shape or distortion that occurred, usually through the application of pressure.

dendritic: Plantlike or skeletal.

dendritic

deposit: A local concentration of a mineral that is economic to mine.

deposition: Action of depositing something.

diagenesis: A process that happens during burial by the accumulation of more tiny rock particles on top of older sediments, creating a harder, more compact rock through pressure.

diapirs: A domed rock formation, in which the rock has moved up to become exposed.

iridescence: (Of a rock or mineral) Having luminous colours that seem to change when seen from different angles.

isotopes: Different forms of a single element.

lava: Hot fluid rock from a volcano; magma that erupts at the Earth's surface.

lava flow: A body of rock formed by a single outpouring of lava through the feeder zone.

lense: A pancake-shaped mass.

lithification: The processes that convert recently deposited sediment into hardened rocks.

lopolith: A mushroom-shaped body, which has layers of rocks in the top part.

lustre: The way that light is reflected off a mineral's surface.

magma: Hot fluid in the Earth's crust or mantle that, when cooled, forms lava and other igneous rocks.

magnetic: Capable of being attracted to a magnet.

mantle: The thick layer of the Earth between the crust and the core.

margin zone: The area around the edges of an intrusion.

massive: Having no particular form or structure.

matrix: The finer-grained material in a rock that surrounds any coarser-grained minerals.

megacrysts: Very large crystals.

metamorphic: Rocks that form from pre-existing rocks due to exposure to a different set of physical conditions, like temperature and pressure.

metamorphism: A process by which rocks are transformed due to changes in temperature and/or pressure.

microcrystalline: Formed of microscopic crystals.

mineralization: The process of converting organic matter wholly or partially into inorganic or mineral matter.

Mohs scale: Scale from 1 to 10 used to determine the hardness of a mineral.

molecules: A group of atoms bonded together.

molten: Liquefied by heat.

mountain-building: Formation of mountains by folding and thrusting of the Earth's crust.

nodule: A small lump, distinct from its surroundings.

nucleus: The positively charged central core of an atom.

nugget: Small lump of precious metal found ready-formed.

occurrence: An isolated location where a mineral has been found.

oceanic ridge: Place at the edges of the oceanic crust where new rocks are being formed through volcanic activity.

octahedron: A three-dimensional shape having eight plane faces.

oil: See petroleum.

oolite: A mass of rounded grains made up of concentric layers.

opaque: Not able to be seen through.

ore deposit: A desirable mineral determined to be of sufficient extent and degree of concentration, capable of being recovered and extracted at a profit.

orthorhombic: (Of a crystal) Having three axes of different lengths, all perpendicular to one another.

orthorhombic

outcrop: Bedrock that sticks up through the overlying cover of glacial debris.

parting: The tendency of crystals to separate along certain planes that are not true cleavage planes.

perfect cleavage: Very clearly observed breaks with smooth, flat planes developed.

petroleum: Synonymous with crude oil; a naturally occurring complex liquid hydrocarbon which can be distilled to produce a range of combustible fuels, petrochemicals, and lubricants.

pipe: A vertical, cylindrical mass of rock, formed in what was the vent of a volcano.

plate tectonics: A theory explaining the structure of the Earth's crust as being created by moving plates.

platy: Broad and flat like a plate.

plugs: A small cylindrical body that is almost or completely vertical in the core of a volcano.

pluton: A general term for any large body of intrusive igneous rock, irrespective of its shape.

pods: Cylindrical shaped mass that is tapered at both ends.

poor cleavage: Poorly developed breaks along well-defined planes of weakness.

porphyritic: A texture, mainly found in volcanic rocks, containing distinct crystalline particles in an otherwise massive rock.

prismatic: Having long and narrow crystals.

pseudomorph: Mineral formation with a crystal shape that is not characteristic of that mineral. A pseudomorph grows in a cavity that is left after another mineral is dissolved or otherwise eliminated, hence the false shape of the new mineral.

pyroclastic: Relating to fragments of rock erupted by a volcano.

radiating aggregates: Masses oriented like spokes in a wheel.

radical: Group of atoms that behave together in a very stable way, thus resisting any chemical changes.

radiolaria: Protozoans that are rich in silica.

radiometric dating: The calculation of age of geologic materials by any one of several methods based on nuclear decay of natural radioactive elements contained in the material.

refraction: The phenomenon of light bending as it passes from one substance to another.

regional metamorphism: The process through which crustal plates collide and the crust buckles, faults, and moves around, essentially creating mountains. The rocks that are pushed downward into deeper levels of the Earth's crust are then exposed to greater temperatures and pressures, changing the minerals to new ones.

reniform: Rounded, kidney-shaped.

resinous: Resembling sap from pine trees.

sectile: Capable of being cut smoothly with a knife.

sediment: The accumulation of weathering products of other rocks.

sedimentary: (Of a rock) Formed from debris deposited by wind or water.

sedimentation: Depositing or formation of sediment.

semimetals: Minerals that are partly metallic and partly non-metallic.

shelf: A rock, ledge of rocks, reef, or sandbank in the sea.

shock wave: A compressional wave of supersonic velocity formed whenever the speed of a body exceeds the ability of the medium to transmit sound; shock waves have a pattern of flow that changes abruptly with corresponding changes in temperature, pressure, and density.

sill: A tabular sheet of igneous rock that is intruded between and parallel to the existing rock layers.

soil: Eroded earth and rock materials sufficiently loosened to allow growth of rooted plants.

specific gravity: A measure of the heaviness of a mineral, as compared to an equal volume of water.

sphenoid: A wedge-shaped crystal with four triangular faces.

splintery fracture: A break that looks like broken wood.

stalactite: Icicle-like structure hanging from the roof of a cave, made from water dripping and depositing calcium salts.

stock: A small intrusion.

streak: The powder left on a piece of porcelain when a mineral is dragged across it; one major characteristic that helps in mineral identification.

striations

striation: Scratches or fine parallel lines.

stylolite: An irregular surface or seam within a rock.

subduction zone: A place on the Earth's crust where two crustal plates collide and the oceanic plate bends down to pass under the continental plate.

subsidence: Sinking of any large part of the Earth's crust relative to another part.

sub-metallic: Somewhat resembling a metal.

swallowtail: A type of twinned crystal common to gypsum, resembling a swallow's tail.

symmetry: Similar parts facing each other head on or around an axis.

tabular: Long and wide but quite thin, like a table.

tabular

tangential: Of or pertaining to a tangent; touching but not intersecting a curve or curved surface.

tarnish: A thin film that coats the exposed surface of a mineral, forming a film that diminishes its shine.

till: Deposits of loose cobbles and boulders left lying around by the last glaciers that crossed the land.

translucent: Partially clear or see-through.

twin plane: A plane in which one crystal is reflected onto its twin.

twinning: When two or more crystals of the same type grow together.

twins: Two or more crystals of the same species grown together in a symmetrical fashion.

ultramafic: Relating to igneous rocks that are formed from minerals very rich in magnesium and iron.

unit: A definable area in which all the rocks are of one type.

uplift: The rising of any part of the crust relative to another part.

vein: A fracture in a rock containing a deposit of minerals or ore.

vent: A near-vertical hole in a volcano.

vitreous: Resembling glass.

volatile: A substance easily evaporated at normal temperatures.

volcanic: Produced by a volcano.

weathering: A group of processes whereby rocks exposed to the atmosphere alter, break down, and eventually crumble into soil.

younging: The direction in which the stratigraphy becomes progressively younger for a particular formation.

zonation: Distribution in bands or regions of distinct character.

Sorrell, Charles A. *A Field Guide and Introduction to the Geology and Chemistry of Rocks and Minerals*. New York: St. Martin's Press, 1973.

Stepanski, Scott. *Resource Guide to Earth Sciences*. Philadelphia: The Academy of Natural Sciences, 1991.

Wilson, Bradley S. "Recent Exploration for Coloured Gemstones in Canada." *The Canadian Gemmologist* 26, no. 2 (2005): 57–63.

Zim, Herbert S. and Paul R. Shaffer. *Rocks and Minerals: A Guide to Familiar Minerals, Gems, Ores and Rocks*. New York: St. Martin's Press, 2001.

Index

A

acicular 10, 92
actinolite 84, 85, 93, 113, 124, 200
alabaster 78, 79, 80, 171
albite 93, 110, 111
alluvial fan 29
almandine 94
amethyst 8, 114, 115
amphibole 13, 84, 85, 91, 96, 124, 128, 164,
    200, 203
amphibolite 85, 97, 182, 200, 201
andalusite 86, 87, 98, 118, 119, 196, 221
andesite 89, 128, 129, 130, 131, 134
andradite 94
anhydrite 79, 171
anorthite 110, 111
anorthosite 140, 141, 169
apatite 12, 82, 83, 99, 132, 134, 148, 203,
    209
Archean age rocks 37
Arctic Platform 37
arkose 178, 179, 180, 182
arsenic 17, 49
arsenide minerals 17
arsenopyrite 43, 48, 49
asbestos 117, 124, 125, 163, 219
ash 27, 28, 73, 130, 131
ash fragments 130
ash tuff 130, 131, 221
atholiths 26, 150
atomic structure 8, 9, 15, 17
augite 93, 112, 113
Axel Heiberg Island 31, 73, 79, 171, 177
axes of symmetry 14, 88, 96, 100, 120

B

Baffin Island 28, 34, 37, 119, 123, 159, 173,
    175, 195, 211
Baker Lake 101, 121, 140, 155, 178, 185,
    187
basalt 27, 28, 89, 91, 93, 97, 104, 113, 115,
    132, 133, 143, 197, 201, 202, 217
batholiths 26, 149
beryl 105, 161
biotite mica 128
black jack 62, 63
bomb 28, 131
borates 18
bort 40, 41
breccia 180, 181

C

calcite crystals 74, 75
calcium 8, 31, 46, 93, 111, 113, 179
calc-silicate 44, 65, 194, 195, 198
carbonado 40, 41
carbonate 18, 30, 31, 74, 76
cataclastic metamorphism 33
chalcopyrite 50–52, 60, 61, 63, 75, 139, 160,
    195, 198
charnockite 206, 207
chart 14, 22, 24, 25, 35
chemical sediments 31
chert 31, 114, 115, 166, 168, 169, 172, 182
chiastolite 86, 87, 196
chlorite 84, 90, 91, 93, 133, 183–185, 200,
    203, 212–214, 216–218, 220
chlorite schist 91, 217
chondrules 222
chromite 105, 147, 152, 163, 218, 219
chrysotile 116, 117, 218
clasts 182–185
clay 29, 79, 173, 176, 183, 188, 189
clay minerals 168, 171, 174, 176, 188, 216
cleavage 9, 12, 13, 88, 90, 106, 221
    distinct 13, 48, 50
    perfect 13, 40, 44, 54, 63, 74, 79, 88, 90,
        97, 98, 100, 106, 108, 120, 124
clinozoisite 92, 93
coal 30, 31, 44, 57, 79, 192, 193
colourless streak 84

237

239

quartzite 34, 101, 114, 182, 208, 214, 215

R

refraction, double 15, 75
rhyolite 47, 89, 130, 131, 134, 136, 139, 183, 217
rip-rap 143, 167
rock crystal 114
rocks
    aluminum-rich 70, 86, 98, 118
    andesite 89, 129–131, 134
    batholithic 26
    biogenic 3, 20, 30, 166, 174
    calcium-rich metamorphic 113
    detrital 30, 31, 35, 172, 188, 190, 225
    evaporite 171, 176
    gas-bearing 30
    gypsum 12, 15, 31, 72, 79, 80, 89, 167, 170, 171, 188, 230
    hornfels 86, 89, 196, 197
    low grade metamorphic 91
    nepheline syenite 103, 158, 159, 161
    permeable 177
    pre-existing metamorphic 33
    regional metamorphic 67, 84, 86, 93
    silica 31, 42, 46, 103, 111, 114, 115, 136, 159, 168, 169, 179, 229
    transitional 151, 157
    volcaniclastic 91
    white quartzite 101
    rock salt 18, 171, 176, 177
    ruby 64

S

salt 18, 31, 54, 64, 72, 73, 79, 167, 171, 176, 177
salt domes 73, 79, 177
salt plugs 177
sandstone 31, 34, 89, 111, 115, 170, 172, 180, 182, 184, 186–190, 215

scapolite 195, 199
schist 44, 65, 85, 89, 91, 94, 95, 97, 106, 111, 114, 118, 208, 212–214, 216, 217
sediments, detrital 30, 31, 35
selenite 78, 79
semimetals 17
sericite 100
serpentine 9, 116, 147, 152, 163, 194, 198, 203, 209, 218, 219
serpentinite 84, 94, 113, 124, 202, 219
shale 31, 86, 100, 169, 176, 184, 185, 188–191, 213, 221
silica 31, 42, 46, 103, 111, 114, 115, 136, 159, 168, 169, 179
silicates 17, 84, 86, 88, 90, 92, 94, 96, 98, 100, 102, 104, 106, 108, 110, 112, 114, 116, 118, 120, 122, 124
sillimanite 87, 98, 118, 119, 204, 206, 211, 216
sillimanite crystals 119
sills 27, 89, 142, 144, 146, 149, 150, 155, 158, 163, 165
silt 29, 30, 172, 181, 190, 191
siltstone 170, 184, 185, 189–191, 221
silver 42, 43, 46–48, 52, 55, 77, 167
skarn 195, 198, 199
slate 50, 220, 221
soapstone 7, 121
sodium 73, 83, 111, 158, 159, 177
spessartine 94
sphalerite 31, 55, 62, 63, 77, 139, 161, 181, 198
spinel 65, 71, 119
stalactites 74, 75
streak 9, 12, 42, 44, 46, 48, 50, 54, 56, 60, 62, 66–68, 72, 75, 84, 90, 97, 113, 116, 118
sulphate 18
sulphide minerals 43, 55, 60, 75, 142, 195, 198, 199
sulphosalts 17
sulphur 17, 175, 192
sunstone 111